Elementary English Course

Contents

INTRODUCTION	Health and the Human Body
GRAMMAR	Articles
GRAMMAR	SVOPT Word Order
PRONUNCIATION	Intonation
GRAMMAR	Past Simple and Past Continuous
GRAMMAR	Common Regular and Irregular Verbs
GRAMMAR	This, That, These, and Those
VOCABULARY	Daily Routines

Answers

Elementary English Course

3.0.1   This unit is called Health and the Human Body. We are going to learn about the following topics:

1. Articles
2. SVOPT Word Order
3. Intonation
4. Past Simple and Past Continuous
5. Common Regular and Irregular Verbs
6. This, That, These, and Those
7. Daily Routines

Exercises

Ex. 3.0.1   **Speaking** Discuss the following questions with a partner or small group:

1. Have you ever been to hospital? Tell me about it.
2. What would you do if a member of your family, or your best friend, had an accident?
3. How healthy are you? How often do you get ill? Do you go to the gym or exercise regularly?
4. What do you like the most / the least about your body? What would you like to change about your body if you could?
5. Would you ever consider having plastic surgery? If yes, what would you have done, and how would you pay for it? If no, why not?
6. What is the name, address and phone number of your dentist?
7. How would you make an appointment with your doctor – in English?
8. How often do you get your hair cut? Where do you get it cut? How much does it cost? Would you recommend your hairdresser? When did you last have a new hairstyle? When are you planning to have a new one? Have you got any tattoos or body piercings? If yes, where are they? Why do people have them?
9. Do you know anyone who is a hypochondriac? Are you one? Tell me more.
10. Do you take vitamin supplements or natural remedies? Do they have any effect?
11. In your opinion, who are the most attractive people in the world? Why are they attractive? What makes a person attractive? Is beauty only skin deep?
12. How would you feel, and how would you handle it, if you lost your… a) hair b) sense of taste c) sight d) hearing e) arms f) legs g) speech?
13. Would you like your body to be cryogenically frozen when you die so that you can perhaps be brought back to life in the future? Why? / Why not?
14. Do you carry a donor card? Would you like to give another person part of your body when you die? Why? / Why not? Should it be compulsory to carry a donor card?
15. Who is the unhealthiest person you know? Have you tried to encourage them to be healthier? Tell me more.
16. If you could swap bodies with somebody else for one day, who would it be? Why? What would you do?

Elementary English Course

Ex. 3.0.2   **Vocabulary** Here are the parts of the body. Translate them into your language and learn them:

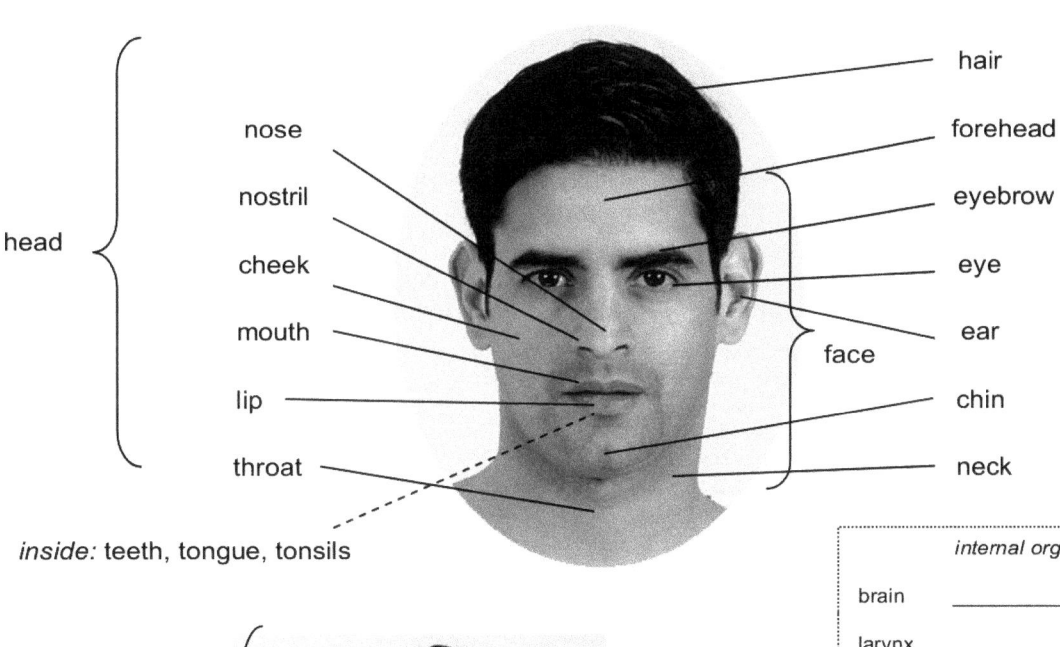

head { nose, nostril, cheek, mouth, lip, throat

face } forehead, eyebrow, eye, ear, chin, neck

hair

inside: teeth, tongue, tonsils

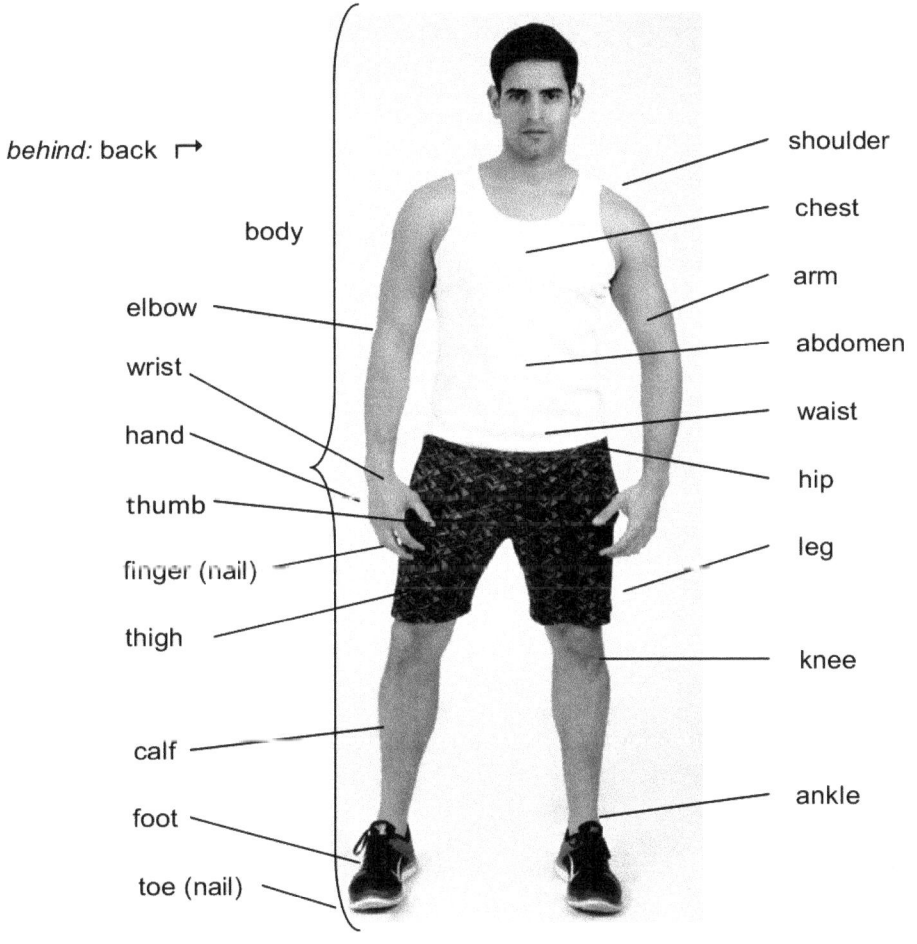

behind: back →

body { elbow, wrist, hand, thumb, finger (nail), thigh, calf, foot, toe (nail) }

shoulder, chest, arm, abdomen, waist, hip, leg, knee, ankle

internal organs:
brain _____
larynx _____
trachea (windpipe) _____
heart _____
lung _____
liver _____
kidney _____
stomach _____
pancreas _____
intestines _____
appendix _____
bladder _____

other parts of the body:
bone _____
skeleton _____
muscle _____
skin _____
vein _____
nerve _____
spine _____
blood _____

Elementary English Course

Ex. 3.0.3 **Speaking** Work with a partner or small group. Study the vocabulary on this page and p.6. Think of some real-life situations where you could use the following functions, then create short dialogues or role plays based on the topic of Health and the Human Body:

- tell
- explain
- warn
- confirm

Ex. 3.0.4 **Writing** Here are 30 words connected with the topic of Health and the Human Body. Translate them into your first language and learn them:

1. toothbrush
2. health
3. emergency
4. illness
5. pharmacy
6. surgery
7. stethoscope
8. stretcher
9. toothpaste
10. hospital
11. dentist
12. injection
13. stitches
14. receptionist
15. waiting room
16. crutch
17. ambulance
18. nurse
19. tablets
20. examination
21. x-ray
22. doctor
23. plaster
24. appointment
25. prescription
26. wheelchair
27. patient
28. accident
29. problem
30. needle

Ex. 3.0.5 **Writing** Translate the health problems into your first language and learn them, then put them into groups below. Note: answers may vary and provoke discussion!

1. infection
2. cut
3. stomach ache
4. broken bone
5. cancer
6. HIV / AIDS
7. headache
8. fever
9. allergy
10. rash
11. toothache
12. migraine
13. sunburn
14. diabetes
15. heart attack
16. cold
17. Parkinson's disease
18. flu
19. leukemia
20. asthma

not serious:	serious:	life-threatening:

Ex. 3.0.6 **Vocabulary** Write the parts of the body:

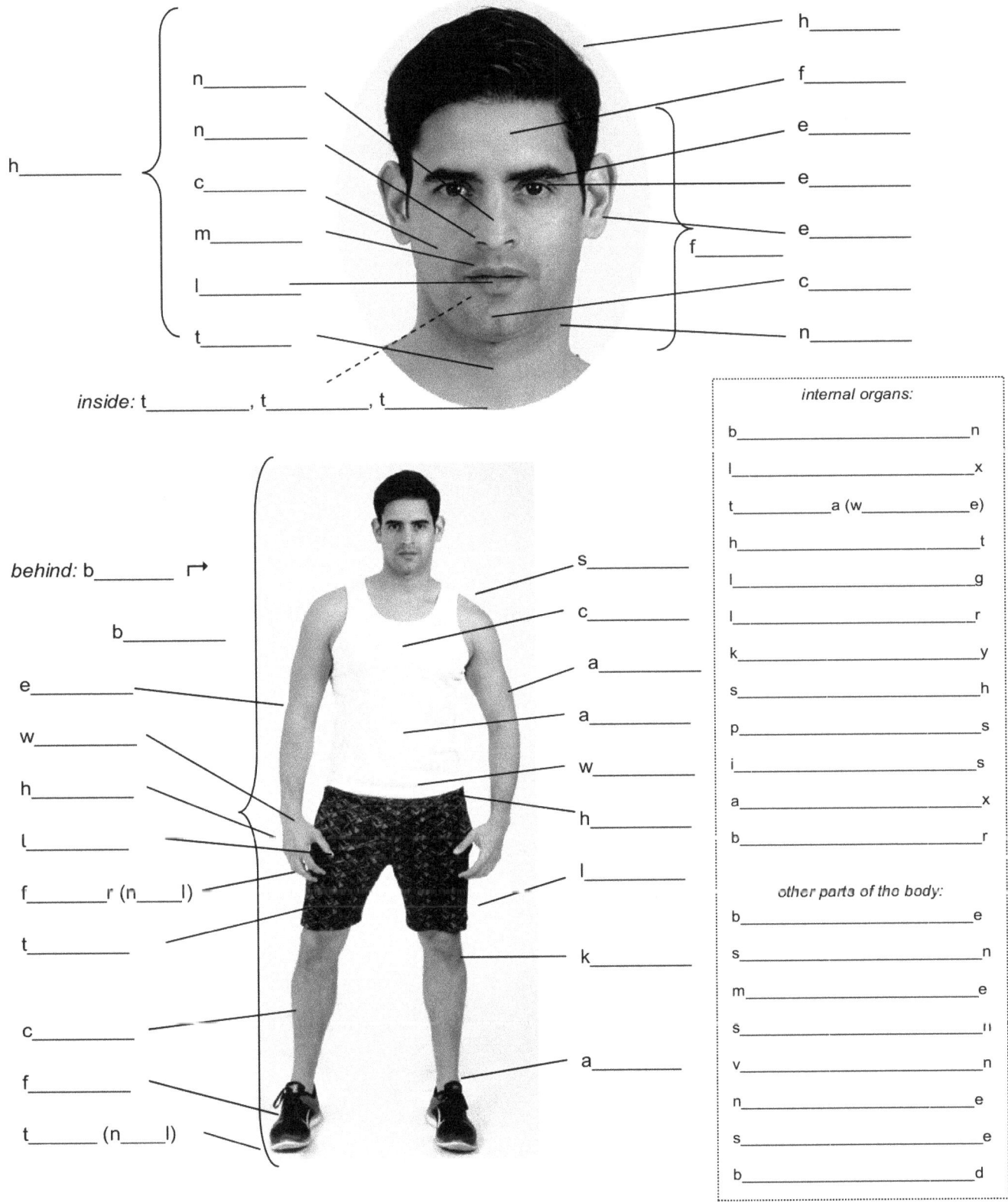

Ex. 3.0.7   **Writing** Draw an outline of a human body and label it with 20 (or more) *external* parts:

Ex. 3.0.8   **Writing** Draw an outline of a human body and label it with 10 (or more) *internal* parts:

Ex. 3.0.9   **Reading** Solve the anagrams and write the names of 20 parts of the body:

1. are _____
2. knec _____
3. osen _____
4. yee _____
5. rottha _____
6. gel _____
7. kelan _____
8. tofo _____
9. grenif _____
10. ram _____

11. daeh _____
12. hoctsma _____
13. oludsreh _____
14. anhd _____
15. techs _____
16. loebw _____
17. ote _____
18. kabc _____
19. thoum _____
20. eekn _____

Ex. 3.0.10   **Reading** Complete the parts of the body with vowel letters:

1. sp __ n __
2. ch __ __ k
3. tr __ ch __ __
4. f __ r __ h __ __ d
5. wr __ st
6. th __ mb
7. t __ __ th
8. br __ __ n
9. k __ dn __ y
10. h __ __ r

11. m __ scl __
12. __ y __ br __ w
13. th __ gh
14. l __ rynx
15. v __ __ n
16. t __ __ n __ __ l
17. n __ str __ l
18. __ nt __ st __ n __ s
19. b __ w __ l
20. l __ v __ r

Ex. 3.0.11   **Speaking & Listening** Complete the table with a partner or small group, then create role plays based on the different patients visiting their doctor. Try to use the functions from Ex. 3.0.3 too:

	Patient & Age:	Symptoms:	Diagnosis:	Treatment:	Result after Two Weeks:
Example:	Mrs. Jones, 44	runny nose	cold	rest; hot honey and lemon drinks	cured / better
1					
2					
3					
4					

For homework, students could write up each patient's notes as a doctor's report, e.g.

"Mrs. Jones came to see me on Monday. She had a runny nose and I diagnosed a cold. I told her to rest and encouraged her to drink hot honey and lemon drinks. After two weeks I saw her again and she confirmed that she felt much better..."

Ex. 3.0.12　　　**Writing**　Write about a memorable visit to your doctor, dentist, or a stay in hospital:

Name: _____　Date: _____

Unit 3.1 Articles

3.1.1   There are only three articles in the English language – **a**, **an** (indefinite articles), and **the** (definite article) – but they cause an enormous amount of confusion among students! They can be difficult to understand because many languages do not include them so they cannot be translated, e.g. Polish, Japanese, and Russian. Articles are **function words**, rather than **content words**, and belong to a larger group of words called **determiners**. Unfortunately, we need to study articles because these words are very common in the English language. In fact, **the** is the most common word in written English, while **a** is #6 and **an** is #32. We often need to put an article before a noun. Which article we use and whether we use one at all depends on the **type of noun** and the **context**:

	Type of Noun:	Example:	Context:	Use this Article:
A	singular countable	book	general	a (before a consonant sound)
B				an (before a vowel sound)
C			specific	the
D	plural	books	general	zero article
E			specific	the
F	uncountable – concrete	water	general	zero article
G			specific	the
H	uncountable – abstract	music	general	zero article
I			specific	the
J	proper	Barcelona	N/A	zero article

If you are unsure about using articles you should check your writing when you finish: look at each noun, think about what **type** it is and the **context**, and whether an article is required – or not.

See also the larger photocopiable version of this table on p.16.

3.1.2   Why do we even need articles anyway? One of the advantages they have is that they introduce a weak stressed syllable with a **schwa sound** right before a content word, which often has a strong stressed first syllable. This helps to emphasis the content word, from which we get meaning, as well as creating the typical rhythm and 'bounce' of spoken English. For example:

o / o o /   o / o /

I'm reading a book.   sounds much better than: I'm reading book.

It sounds more like English.

3.1.3   As you can see from the table above, if the noun is singular and countable there must be an article before it. If the context is general, you can use a or an. We use an before a noun that begins with a vowel sound, e.g.

A: I need a book.   *noun begins with a consonant sound = use a*
B: I need an egg.   *noun begins with a vowel sound = use an*

In both sentences the context is general – we don't know anything about the book or the egg. It is the first time they are mentioned = **first mention**.

In the following sentence, because we now know about the two nouns (book and egg), the context becomes specific and we use the.

C: This is the book I need.
C: This is the egg I need.

If a countable noun is plural and the context is general or it is first mention, we don't use an article. This is called "zero article" – when there is no article, e.g.

D: I like books.

But if the context is specific – the noun is defined in some way – then we use the:

E: The books in this library are really old.

The same applies to uncountable nouns – both real (concrete):

F: I use water every day.   *general context, i.e. any water = no article*
G: The water is very hot.   *specific context, i.e. this water = use the*

...and abstract:

H: I love music.   *general context, i.e. all music = no article*
I: The music in this club is great. *specific context = use the*

Proper nouns are words which always start with a capital letter, like the names of people ("Eric Harrison"), cities ("Birmingham"), countries ("Mexico"), companies ("McDonalds"), products ("Coke Zero"), days ("Monday"), months ("December"), etc. We do not usually put an article before a proper noun.
Exception 1: when the proper noun is made up of an adjective + noun (e.g. "United" = adjective + "Kingdom" = noun) we need to use the definite article: "I live in the United Kingdom."

J: Barcelona is such a beautiful city.   NOT The Barcelona...

Exception 2: We use the definite article with plural place names, e.g. the Bahamas. If you are still not sure which article to use with each noun in your text, use the flow chart on p.17.

3.1.4   Some example errors:

"I live in the house in Bristol."
Use a because there is more than one house in Bristol!

"What's a phone number for the swimming pool?"
Use the because the swimming pool has got one specific phone number.

"Music was too loud so we had to leave."
Use the because in this context music is specific – the music in that place.

3.1.5   We use the when the noun is specific or known to each person in the conversation. For example:

I went to the new cinema on Leyland Street last night.
It is a specific cinema – not just any cinema. We cannot say "...a cinema on Leyland Street" because it is very unlikely for there to be more than one!

Let's switch on the TV and watch Coronation Street.
The person or people I am talking to know about the TV and can probably see it because we are all in the same room.

We also use the before **superlative adjectives** and **ordinal numbers**:

It is the best TV programme.   *best is the superlative form of the adjective 'good'*

I'm the first person to finish!   *first is an ordinal number (of one)*

Interestingly, the word the has two different pronunciations:

- before a consonant sound: th   with an **embedded schwa sound**
- before a vowel sound   thii   with a short ii sound

3.1.6   We can use the determiner some before plural and uncountable nouns instead of zero article:

I would like spaghetti. > I would like some spaghetii.

It sounds better because the weak stressed word some has a schwa sound and this extra weak syllable improves the rhythm and 'bounce' of the sentence. It sounds more naturally English:

o o   /   o / o   o o   /   o   o / o
I would like spaghetti. > I would like some spaghetti.

If the sentence is negative or a question form we use any instead of some:

Would you like any spaghetti? / No, I wouldn't like any spaghetti.

3.1.7   We use a when we talk about frequency or quantity:

'Once a week.'
'Three times a day.'
'£1.15 pence a litre.'

3.1.8   If the thing has one or more modifier before it – e.g. an adjective or an intensifier – the article goes before the first modifier:

'It was a great party.'
'My grandma had a really lovely day.'

3.1.9   We can use a possessive adjective (e.g. my, your, our, etc.) instead of an article – but never with an article! – when the noun belongs to somebody:

This is a book. > This is my book.   ~~This is a my book.~~ / ~~This is her the book.~~

Or we can use different determiners, e.g. this, that, these, those instead of an article – but never with an article:

I want a book. > I want this book.   ~~I want this a book.~~ / ~~I want these the books.~~

See also the information on p.18 regarding articles and how to use them.

Use of Articles in English

*We know which article to use because of the **type of noun** and the **context** – general or specific:*

- **singular countable nouns**
  - general / not known / first mention
    - begin with a consonant sound   book → use a
    - begin with a vowel sound   apple → use an
  - specific / known / later mention → use the

- **plural nouns**   books   **and uncountable nouns**
  - concrete   bread
  - abstract   music
  - general / unknown / first mention → zero article
  - specific / known / later mention → use the

- **proper nouns**   Italy → zero article

For example:

I read a book yesterday.
I ate an apple yesterday.
The book was great.
The apple was delicious.
I love reading books.
They eat bread every day.
Music is important to me.
I love the books you gave me.
They ate the fresh bread you bought.
The music of Bach is wonderful.
My brother lives in Italy.

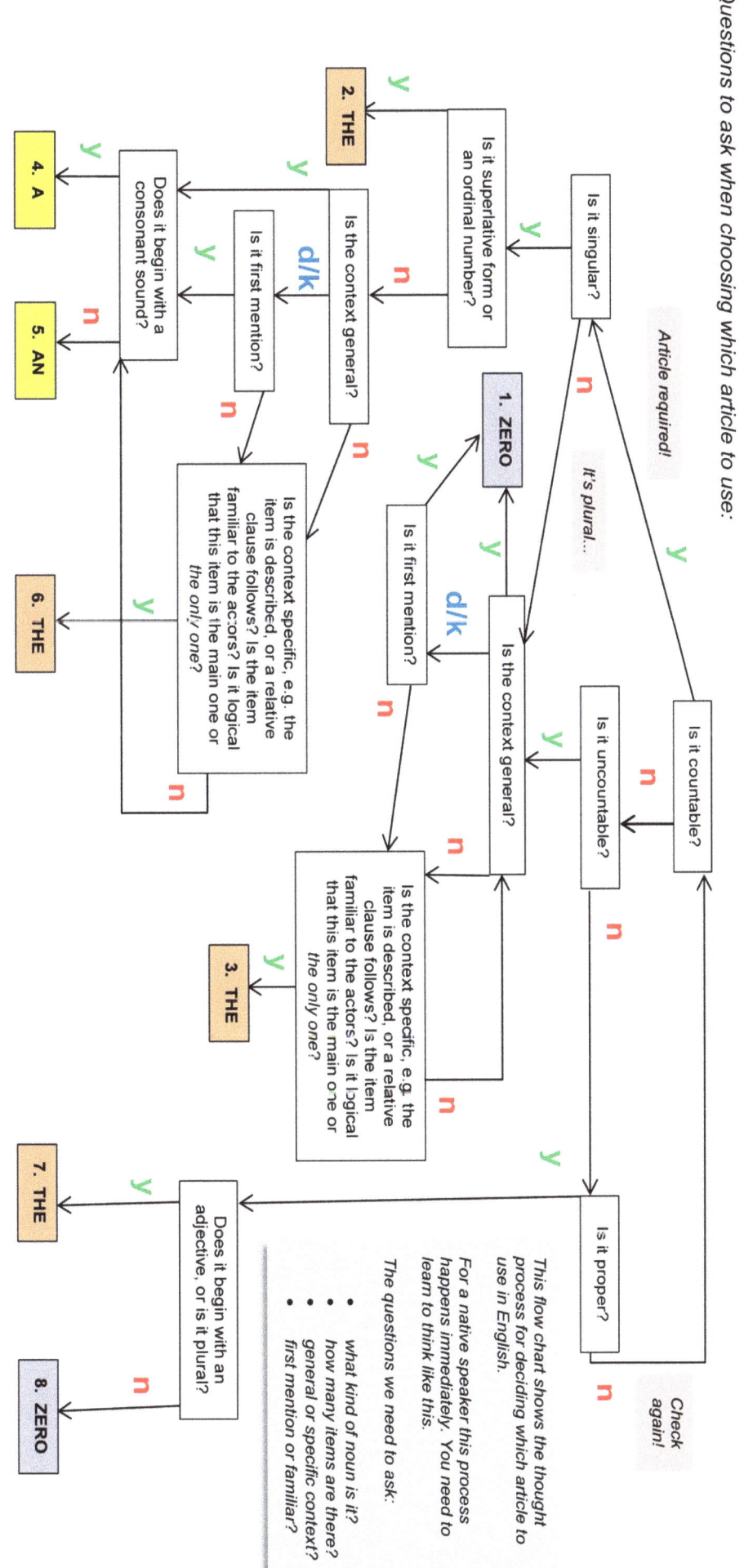

Understanding Articles in English

How we talk about nouns (things):

	countable	uncountable	abstract
singular	(shop)	(food)	(love)
plural	(shops)		
	(book)		
	(table)		
	(United Kingdom)		
	common	proper	

a, an (1)
- singular countable nouns
- unknown / first mention
- general
- **an** is the same as **a** but we use it before a vowel sound

the (1 or more)
- countable nouns – singular or plural
- known / later mentions
- specific things
- specific uncountable / plural nouns
- specific abstract nouns
- use **the** when you both know what is being talked about
- use **the** before superlative adjectives and ordinal numbers
- pronounced *thi* before vowel sounds

no article ("or "some")
- uncountable nouns*
- plural nouns
- abstract nouns*
- proper nouns
- things when you are talking in general

- We often need to write an article before a noun – *but not always!*
- There are only 3 articles – **a**, **an**, and **the** – but they cause a lot of errors
- **the** is the most common word in written English; **a** is #6 and **an** is #32 (*Talk a Lot Foundation Course* p.3.9)
- Some languages don't have articles, e.g. Polish; in English we need them to help make the rhythm and give more information
- Use **some** with plural countable nouns and with uncountable nouns; use **any** in question and negative forms
- Some nouns can be both countable and uncountable depending on the situation, e.g. cheese
- An article goes before a noun modifier, e.g. an adjective or intensifier, e.g. "a horse"; "a big horse"; "a really big horse"
- We can use a possessive adjective (e.g. my, your, our, etc.) or a determiner (e.g. this, that, these, those) instead of an article

Unfortunately, there are a lot of exceptions to these rules! You should read English often to see the repeating patterns

Exercises

Ex. 3.1.1 **Writing** Which indefinite article should we write in front of the following words - 'a' or 'an'?

1. _____ chair
2. _____ girl
3. _____ school
4. _____ egg
5. _____ hour
6. _____ apple
7. _____ exam
8. _____ hospital
9. _____ year
10. _____ university
11. _____ address
12. _____ ear
13. _____ sheep
14. _____ tie
15. _____ union
16. _____ orange
17. _____ ice cream
18. _____ pencil
19. _____ umbrella
20. _____ shoe
21. _____ number
22. _____ heater
23. _____ interview
24. _____ appliance
25. _____ heir
26. _____ computer
27. _____ bag
28. _____ octopus
29. _____ ewe
30. _____ fridge

Ex. 3.1.2 **Writing** Complete the four gaps in each question with a, an, the, and - (zero article):

1. - Do you like a)_____ Copenhagen?
   - Yes, I do. b)_____ first time I came here I stayed in
   c)_____ tiny guest house. The owner had
   d)_____ enormous dog!

2. I read a)_____ good book last week.
   b)_____ book was by Alfredo Montessauri. He is
   c)_____ Italian writer. I got a lot of d)_____
   pleasure from it.

3. a)_____ Sarah works at b)_____ bank.
   c)_____ bank is forty miles from her home. She has
   d)_____ eighty-minute commute each way.

4. I really love a)_____ fish, and b)_____ fish
   in this restaurant is superb. I'm looking forward to eating
   c)_____ big juicy fish in d)_____ hour from
   now!

5. I went to a)_____ swimming pool yesterday.
   b)_____ little boy fell over and had to have
   c)_____ treatment on his leg. d)_____
   assistant said that he would be OK.

6. - I can meet you tomorrow.
   - Have you got a)_____ time?
   -Yes. I've got b)_____ appointment with
   c)_____ builder at eleven, but I can change
   d)_____ time.

7. - Don't be late for a)_____ work, or
   b)_____ manager will be angry with you.
   - OK, I will use c)_____ alarm clock and also ask
   d)_____ friend to give me a wake-up call at six o'clock.

8. - I bought a)_____ blue guitar on Wednesday.
   - The one I saw? Super! Can you play it?
   - No, but I'm having b)_____ few lessons with
   c)_____ old guy called d)_____ Barry.

9. - Have you seen a)_____ old jumper anywhere?
    - Is it b)_____ one with the blue collar?
    - Yes, and it's got c)_____ orange stripes.
    - It's over there, under d)_____ pile of cushions.

10. I went to a)_____ post office yesterday to post b)_____ parcel. It cost about c)_____ twenty pounds, which I thought was d)_____ extortionate amount of money.

11. One of our neighbours is a)_____ guy who hails from b)_____ Finland. He is c)_____ interpreter who works at d)_____ same firm as my uncle.

12. - Let's put a)_____ kettle on and have b)_____ nice cup of tea.
    - Good idea! There's c)_____ open packet of chocolate biccies in the cupboard! What shall we drink to?
    - To d)_____ friendship!

13. I haven't been to a)_____ work for fourteen days because I've had b)_____ really bad back. I got c)_____ awful pain at the base of my spine and d)_____ doctor told me that I had to rest.

14. - Shall we meet at a)_____ Burger King, or b)_____ new coffee house in Market Street?
    - They've got c)_____ offer on at the moment – if you buy d)_____ latte, you get two free mini doughnuts.

15. Geoffrey Chaucer was a)_____ English poet and philosopher who is considered by b)_____ scholars to be c)_____ greatest writer of the Middle Ages. *The Canterbury Tales* is d)_____ wonderfully rich piece of literature.

16. - Is there a)_____ free table anywhere in this café?
    - Yes, look – b)_____ table by the window is available. Oh – hang on – c)_____ old feller's just sat down.
    - Just our d)_____ luck!

Ex. 3.1.3   **Reading**   Print the worksheet on p.21 titled 'Noun Categories' and follow the instructions.

Ex. 3.1.4   **Reading**   Print the worksheet on p.22 titled 'Use of Articles in English – 40 Question Quiz' and follow the instructions.

Elementary English Course

Noun Categories

Tick ✓ the nouns in each box that match the category:

singular countable nouns:

book	buses
orange juice	Microsoft
information	children
watch	Monday
t-shirts	love
furniture	umbrella
clock	rugby
beef	transport
Richard	socks
work	Europe

plural nouns:

book	buses
orange juice	Microsoft
information	children
watch	Monday
t-shirts	love
furniture	umbrella
clock	rugby
beef	transport
Richard	socks
work	Europe

uncountable nouns:

book	buses
orange juice	Microsoft
information	children
watch	Monday
t-shirts	love
furniture	umbrella
clock	rugby
beef	transport
Richard	socks
work	Europe

proper nouns:

book	buses
orange juice	Microsoft
information	children
watch	Monday
t-shirts	love
furniture	umbrella
clock	rugby
beef	transport
Richard	socks
work	Europe

common nouns:

book	buses
orange juice	Microsoft
information	children
watch	Monday
t-shirts	love
furniture	umbrella
clock	rugby
beef	transport
Richard	socks
work	Europe

abstract nouns:

book	buses
orange juice	Microsoft
information	children
watch	Monday
t-shirts	love
furniture	umbrella
clock	rugby
beef	transport
Richard	socks
work	Europe

Elementary English Course

Use of Articles in English – 40 Question Quiz

*Write **a**, **an**, or **the** in each gap, or put **-** to mean zero article*

1. He was born in _____ August.
2. John sells _____ bikes every day.
3. Do you want _____ spaghetti today?
4. It was _____ hottest day ever!
5. He prefers _____ Adidas.
6. I put _____ unopened letters over there.
7. Is _____ clock slow, or is it me?
8. Would you like _____ apricot?
9. We were moved by _____ kindness that he showed.
10. I got _____ puppy yesterday.

11. We've booked _____ taxi for you.
12. Do you believe in _____ justice for everybody?
13. Please would you put _____ rubbish out?
14. What about _____ beef for dinner?
15. Is _____ milk semi-skimmed or skimmed?
16. It seems that _____ mobiles are getting bigger rather than smaller!
17. Do you fancy _____ omelette?
18. Has _____ power come back on yet?
19. I didn't know that _____ dictionary belonged to you.
20. Have you eaten _____ chocolate from Grandma?

21. Both of us took _____ umbrella just in case.
22. We'll ask her for _____ information tomorrow.
23. There were _____ toys everywhere!
24. It's so important that you tell me _____ truth about them.
25. These are _____ channels that I watch most often.
26. He lived on _____ Porter Road when I used to know him.
27. Surprisingly, _____ unemployment had fallen again.
28. I need _____ new kettle, because this one is broken.
29. Can you bring me all _____ empty coffee cups, please?
30. You are _____ first person I have truly loved!

31. We'll be upset if he gets _____ infection.
32. Be careful! It's made of _____ glass.
33. How essential is _____ quality to you?
34. You need to replace _____ printer paper.
35. We start to develop _____ teeth when only a few months old.
36. She found _____ pen outside.
37. I don't like _____ peanut butter.
38. He was pleased with _____ poetry that he had written.
39. I told them about _____ Amanda.
40. Our swimming costumes were dry, but _____ children's weren't.

Ex. 3.1.5   **Writing** Remember the main point: we know which article to use because of the type of noun and the context – general or specific. Look at the summary of rules for using articles in English from 3.1.1:

	Type of Noun:	Example:	Context:	Use this Article:
A	singular countable	book	general	a (before a consonant sound)
B				an (before a vowel sound)
C			specific	the
D	plural	books	general	zero article
E			specific	the
F	uncountable – concrete	water	general	zero article
G			specific	the
H	uncountable – abstract	music	general	zero article
I			specific	the
J	proper	Barcelona	N/A	zero article

i) Underline the noun in each sentence. Say what kind of noun it is
ii) Write **a**, **an**, or **the** in each gap, or put **-** to mean zero article
iii) Write a letter A-J to show which rule the sentence follows

Type of Noun: *Rule:*

a) Do you often listen to _____ music?
b) He said _____ new employees were wonderful.
c) It was _____ second time I had asked you.
d) Is _____ chewing gum allowed?
e) I watched _____ good film yesterday.
f) She lived in _____ Paris.
g) I downloaded _____ app last week.
h) He often bakes _____ cakes.
i) I would like _____ biggest potato.
j) He always drinks _____ Coca-Cola.
k) I was surprised by _____ progress we made.
l) He has bought _____ new car.
m) She thought that _____ rice was a bit undercooked.
n) I wonder why _____ children love to play.
o) I ate _____ egg yesterday.
p) He didn't have _____ patience to be a teacher.
q) I showed her _____ red socks that I had bought.
r) We have already spent _____ money you gave us.
s) I believe that _____ perseverance is important.
t) He has got _____ short brown hair.

Ex. 3.1.6   **Writing** Follow the instructions from Ex. 3.1.5:

Type of Noun: *Rule:*

a) He needs to cut _____ grass.
b) He looks similar to _____ Darren.
c) She doesn't like _____ ice cream.
d) I used _____ green pen.
e) She is looking for _____ work.
f) Would you like _____ orange?
g) This is _____ second photo that he took.
h) We appreciate _____ dedication that you have shown.
i) I think _____ students should always work hard.
j) We arrived on _____ Tuesday.
k) We'll get _____ petrol later on.
l) I didn't have _____ courage that I needed.

m) Sometimes _____ life is hard. _____ _____
n) I put on _____ coat and went out. _____ _____
o) I don't usually get _____ colds. _____ _____
p) We suggested _____ idea to her. _____ _____
q) They preferred _____ leather furniture. _____ _____
r) Did you understand _____ assignments from yesterday? _____ _____
s) She picked up _____ book and started to read it. _____ _____
t) Are _____ chips ready yet? _____ _____

Ex. 3.1.7 **Reading** a) Read the text, which has a gap before every noun. Complete the gaps with **a, an, the,** or **-** (**zero article**):

Yesterday 1.[____] Ellen went to 2.[____] new clothes shop on 3.[____] Bude Street and bought 4.[____] new dress. 5.[____] dress was light green and had 6.[____] white collar. She also went to 7.[____] supermarket and bought 8.[____] groceries. She needed to get 9.[____] chocolate cake and 10.[____] candles for 11.[____] birthday party on 12.[____] Monday. On the way home she had 13.[____] idea and phoned 14.[____] friend. 15.[____] Mandy is 16.[____] florist who works near 17.[____] health centre. 18.[____] Ellen asked 19.[____] Mandy to order 20.[____] flowers.

b) Look at the 7 statements below and say which one applies to each article in the text:

A. We use **a** or **an** because the noun is singular, countable, and in a general context. It is first mention.

B. We use **the** because the noun is used again – after first mention. We are already familiar with it.

C. We use **the** because it is logical that there is only one of these nouns, so it is something specific.

D. We use **the** because the noun is something specific or something familiar to us.

E. We do not use an article (**zero article**) because the noun is a proper noun.

F. We do not use an article (**zero article**) because the noun is plural or uncountable and in a general context.

G. We use a possessive adjective (e.g. **my / her**) because it is clear that the noun is something that belongs to somebody or is closely connected with them.

1. _____
2. _____
3. _____
4. _____
5. _____
6. _____
7. _____
8. _____
9. _____
10. _____

11. _____
12. _____
13. _____
14. _____
15. _____
16. _____
17. _____
18. _____
19. _____
20. _____

Elementary English Course

Unit 3.2 SVOPT Word Order

3.2.1 Word order in a sentence in English is fairly strict compared to other languages. We often use SVOPT word order in a sentence:

S	V	O	P	T
subject	verb	object	place	time
e.g. I, you, we, Jenny		noun phrase	adverbial of place	adverbial of time

For example:

S	V	O	P	T
subject	verb	object	place	time
Jenny	ate	a sandwich	in the kitchen	last night.

This is the order in which English native speakers want to get their information. We generally want to know:

1st	who does the action	**S**ubject
2nd	what they do	**V**erb
3rd	what they do it to	**O**bject
4th	where they do it	**P**lace
5th	when they do it	**T**ime

3.2.2 It is possible to put the time phrase first in the sentence, if you want to emphasise that piece of information:

T	S	V	O	P
time	subject	verb	object	place
Last night	Jenny	ate	a sandwich	in the kitchen.

However, it is better to start with the subject so that we establish WHO is doing the action first. We also get time information from the verb tense. For example, by using the past tense verb 'ate' we understand immediately that the action happened in finished time, in the past. This time information is sufficient until we get final confirmation of the exact time at the end of the sentence: 'last night'.

3.2.3 However, changing the word order in other ways is not permitted in English. For example, the following sentences would be incorrect:

V	O	S	P	T
Ate	a sandwich	Jenny	in the kitchen	last night.

P	S	V	T	O
In the kitchen	Jenny	ate	last night	a sandwich.

They just sound like jumbled up sentences, rather than English. It may be that the person listening can work out what you are saying because all the keywords are present and they are able to 'unjumble' them in their mind as you speak, but it makes a lot of extra work for your listener, who is rather expecting to hear the information presented in SVOPT order.

3.2.4   Not every verb has an object, so sometimes this part of SVOPT will be blank. They are called **intransitive verbs**. For example:

S	V	O	P	T
subject	verb	object	place	time
Jenny	goes	-	to Birmingham	every Friday.

The verb 'go' does not have an object. It is intransitive, so the **O** part of SVOPT is blank.

3.2.5   Similarly, we do not need to include every part of SVOPT word order in every sentence. It is the order that is important and should be followed:

S	V	O	P	T
subject	verb	object	place	time
Jenny	ate	a sandwich.	-	last night.

3.2.6   We can easily turn a SVOPT sentence into a compound sentence but using a conjunction such as:

Jenny ate a sandwich in the kitchen last night...

and	= addition	e.g.	...**and** then read a book.
but	= contrast	e.g.	...**but** she didn't enjoy it.
because	= reason	e.g.	...**because** she felt hungry.
so	= result	e.g.	...**so** she wouldn't feel hungry in the night.

Exercises

Ex. 3.2.1   **Writing** Write 10 sentences with SVOPT word order. You don't need to include an object each time:

     subject   verb   object   place   time

1. _____
2. _____
3. _____
4. _____
5. _____
6. _____
7. _____
8. _____
9. _____
10. _____

Ex. 3.2.2   **Writing** Complete the worksheets on pp.29-32: *Make a Sentence with SVOPT – Subject Verb Object Place Time 1-4*.

Ex. 3.2.3   **Writing** Complete the worksheets on pp.33-34: *Sentence Building with SVOPT Word Order 1-2*.

Ex. 3.2.4   **Writing** Complete the worksheet on p.35: *Practice with SVOPT-R Word Order*.

Elementary English Course

Make a Sentence with SVOPT – Subject Verb Object Place Time 1

SVOPT (Subject Verb Object Place Time) is a very common form of word order in English. Complete the gaps in the sentences with your own words:

SUBJECT	VERB	OBJECT	PLACE	TIME
1._____	will open	2._____	on the market	at 6am tomorrow.
We	3._____	holidays	4._____	every year.
Nelly	has married	5._____	at St Paul's church	6._____
7._____	collects	8._____	from nursery	after work.
Neil	9._____	a cake	10._____	last night.
Eddie	draws	11._____	in his notebook	12._____
13._____	's been chatting	14._____	in the car park	for half an hour.
I	15._____	my laptop	16._____	each day.
Me and Bill	planted	17._____	in the garden	18._____
19._____	will tidy up	20._____	in the flat	by the end of the week

Make a Sentence with SVOPT – Subject Verb Object Place Time 2

SVOPT (Subject Verb Object Place Time) is a very common form of word order in English. Complete the gaps in the sentences with your own words:

SUBJECT	VERB	OBJECT	PLACE	TIME
1._____	closed	2._____	in the dining room	ten minutes ago.
A guy	3._____	my car	4._____	earlier today.
Mrs Stevens	mends	5._____	at the community centre	6._____
7._____	has been packing	8._____	in her bedroom	most of the afternoon.
The boss	9._____	his team	10._____	at 4pm.
My dog	chases	11._____	in the park	12._____
13._____	bit	14._____	on the arm	last night.
I	15._____	the documents	16._____	tomorrow morning.
They	have to clean	17._____	in the kitchen	18._____
19._____	finish	20._____	at the factory	at 6 o'clock.

Make a Sentence with SVOPT – Subject Verb Object Place Time 3

SVOPT (Subject Verb Object Place Time) is a very common form of word order in English. Rearrange the words in each row to make a sentence with SVOPT order:

#					
1.	raised	in class	Lenny	on Monday	his hand
2.	in the living room	my book	I	every day	read
3.	now	'm watching	on my computer	I	a good film
4.	buys	Katy	every week	some grapes	at the greengrocer's
5.	today	his paper	's presented	at the university	he
6.	is wearing	at the moment	she	on her right arm	her watch
7.	all the walls	this week	in our bedroom	have painted	we
8.	her breakfast	every morning	Penny	in front of the telly	eats
9.	later	we	outside the fish and chip shop	will meet	you
10.	at the school concert	the boys	yesterday	some beautiful carols	sang

Elementary English Course

Make a Sentence with SVOPT – Subject Verb Object Place Time 4

SVOPT (Subject Verb Object Place Time) is a very common form of word order in English. Rearrange the words in each row to make a sentence with SVOPT order:

#					
1.	to Florida	we	our flights	have booked	this morning
2.	two coffees	every day at 8.30am	he	at his desk	has
3.	to the station	took	on Saturday evening	we	a taxi
4.	charity cards	I	once a year	in the shopping centre	sell
5.	my hair	will cut	in the salon	in a minute	Joe
6.	in class	Stephanie	a lot of questions	every day	asks
7.	a handbag	a thief	this week	has stolen	from my mother's car
8.	a few minutes ago	their bags	up the stairs	carried	my friends
9.	in the sink	the girls	their hair	twice a week	wash
10.	're going to play	at 2pm	on the playing field	we	hockey

Sentence Building with SVOPT Word Order 1

Write ten different sentences using SVOPT word order and following the prompts below. You **must not** use any of the prompt words, e.g.

1. The bus driver bought four lettuces at the supermarket yesterday.

	Subject:	Verb:	Object:	Place:	Time:
1.	profession		green		
2.		present perfect		relaxing	
3.	group		cold		
4.		past continuous		stressful	
5.	animal		expensive		
6.		future perfect		empty	
7.	female		beautiful		
8.		past simple		crowded	
9.	male		sweet		
10.		future continuous		old	

Sentence Building with SVOPT Word Order 2

Write ten different sentences using SVOPT word order and following the prompts below. You **must not** use any of the prompt words, e.g.

1. An optimistic monkey placed three bananas on the checkout two minutes ago.

	Subject:	Verb:	Object:	Place:	Time:
1.	formal		plural	quiet	
2.		present perfect continuous	smooth		
3.	organisation			dirty	
4.		present simple			
5.	young		unattractive		
6.		past perfect		noisy	
7.	object		collectable		
8.		future perfect continuous		lonely	
9.	old		delicious		
10.		present continuous			cramped

Practice with SVOPT-R Word Order

a) Write a sentence using SVOPT-R word order. Note the tense and auxiliary verb(s) above:

Tense:

Auxiliary Verb(s):

Subject	Verb	Object	Place	Time	Reason
who	what (action)	what (thing)	where	when	why

b) Write wh- questions and short answers based on the sentence:

Question: Short Answer:

1. Who _____ ? _____
2. What _____ ? _____
3. What _____ ? _____
4. Where _____ ? _____
5. When _____ ? _____
6. Why _____ ? _____

c) Write yes / no questions and short answers based on the sentence:

7. _____ ?   Positive Answer: _____

8. _____ ?   Negative Answer: _____

Unit 3.3 Intonation

3.3.1   Along with the phonetic alphabet, sentence stress, and connected speech, intonation is an important element in learning English pronunciation. Read the information on the following two pages and check that you understand it. You could discuss it with a partner or small group, and be sure to ask your teacher to explain anything you don't understand.

3.3.2   Study the table of *21 English Sounds and Words where Intonation Changes the Meaning* on p.42. There are some short sounds and words in English that have different meanings depending on the intonation. Practise saying them out loud. How many are familiar to you? How many are the same or similar in your first language? See how many you can hear when you are listening to real English conversations. You could create role plays with a partner where you use a number of these sounds or words.

Exercises

Ex. 3.3.1   **Writing** Complete the exercises on p.40.

Elementary English Course

Intonation

1. In short, intonation means the ups and downs of the voice in a sentence. Good pronunciation involves three elements: sentence stress (the sound spine), connected speech (connecting syllables, not speaking word by word), and intonation. Varied intonation is more interesting than robotic, monotonous speech, and therefore easier and more appealing to listen to. For example, when reading aloud we should aim to "lift the words from the page" using intonation, rather than reading in a flat boring voice.

Stress is non-negotiable – the sound spine must be heard clearly – and connected speech is a must if you want to sound natural. But stress and connected speech are not enough – we need to use intonation. For example, we could have correct stress and connected speech, but still sound flat, dull, and emotionless. Without hearing emotion we cannot be sure of the speaker's intention. English intonation is more familiar to speakers of some languages than others, e.g. European students of English may find English intonation patterns more familiar than speakers from the Middle East or the Far East. However, many non-English speakers of English would agree that English intonation (and stress) seem "too much" – too exaggerated – when compared with their language.

2. Let's say that we are clear about the sound spine of our sentence and we are using connected speech. What about intonation? Standard (neutral) intonation in a statement (not a question) usually involves going on a journey: up the mountain and back down again. We usually go up around the middle of the sentence, and back down at the end. We must have closure. Let's take an example of a short sentence. We go up in the middle, either: a) at a clause break, e.g.

I went to the post office, because I needed to buy stamps.

or b) on the key concept word, e.g.

I met my friend in the park. ("friend" is the key concept word – it is the main point of the sentence)

In a longer sentence, or a list, there will be more ups and downs. We have to decide which specific words or phrases are the most important in our communication. By "going up" on them we give them emphasis, e.g.

I met my friend with his aunt and brother in the park.

3. Intonation in questions usually depends on the kind of question:

a) For yes/no questions – we go up at the end (rising intonation). The listener feels compelled to answer, because we need closure. For example,

Do you want a lift home?

b) For wh- questions (what, where, when, etc.) – we go down at the end (falling intonation). For example:

Where has Tony gone?

c) When the speaker uses a question tag, they can go up if they want to check some information, e.g.

The concert starts at eight, doesn't it?

d) ...and down if they are making a general statement and believe that the listener will agree, e.g.

We've had a lovely day, haven't we?

We can add extra emphasis when replying to questions, depending on what part of the sentence the speaker asked about. In the sentence below there are seven possible wh- questions that could be asked.

John	rode	his bike	to the city lake	quickly	yesterday,	because he was late.
who	what – action	what – object	where, which	how	when	why

For example, if somebody asked: "Who rode their bike to the city lake?" you could put extra emphasis on the name in the answer, by going up on the word "John": John rode his bike to the city lake. *or* John did.

Elementary English Course

Other intonation techniques include:

- Rising intonation at the end of a statement when we want to continue without being interrupted, e.g.

    I wanted to get some rice at the supermarket. You know, the one on the corner. And it was closed, so...

- When making a list we use rising-falling intonation, e.g.

    Jennifer bought a pencil, a pencil sharpener, some pens, a ruler, and a new bag for school.

Be sure to get that closure at the end!

Function words are usually unstressed in standard English pronunciation, but we can use intonation to give them extra emphasis – to make our point. Each function word has a **strong form** and **a weak form**, so we can use the strong form if we want to **emphasise** that word. For example, the weak form of the auxiliary verb "have" is uhv, while the strong form is Hav – i.e. we hear the strong vowel sound a in the strong form, but in the weak form it is reduced to a **schwa sound**. Here is a sentence with neutral (normal, standard) intonation:

I've finished doing my homework. (general statement – note the normal rise and fall)

...while here is the same sentence but with specific intonation:

I have finished doing my homework. (I'm confirming the news that my homework is finished – stop nagging!)

4. Another important use of intonation is to show mood, which helps to express intention and meaning. There are several invaluable tools in the **intonation toolbox** and each one is adjusted to convey mood, for example:

tone of voice	pitch	extra emphasis on content words	volume	rhythm	speed	pausing (for effect)
angry	higher	yes	louder	intact	faster	yes
sad	lower	no	quieter	broken	slower	no

...and so on. An emotion like anger is a **high-energy emotion** and the speaker demands that the listener hears them clearly. The intonation toolbox enables this. On the other hand, sadness is a **low-energy emotion** and the speaker may be less focused on whether anybody is listening. The intonation tools used reflects this intention.

Of course, tone also depends on the **personality** of the individual person. For example, each person will "sound upset" in a different way. Furthermore, some people – typically men – will have a lower **pitch range** than others – typically women and children.

5. There are a number of short words and sounds that change their meanings completely depending on the intonation (see p.42). If we do not use intonation, or use the wrong kind, our meaning might not be clear and communication may fail. For example:

sound / word:	rising	flat	falling	rising-falling
oh	I'm interested	I'm annoyed	I'm disappointed	I understand at last
OK	Do you agree?	I'm frustrated / stop talking	I accept something	I'm happy to agree
yes	Tell me more / Can I help?	Please stop talking	I agree / I accept something	I strongly agree / sarcasm
no	I didn't know that	Refusal –no discussion	Standard negative reply	It's fine / I don't mind

Elementary English Course

Intonation – Exercises

1. What is... a) sentence stress, b) connected speech, c) intonation?

2. Draw the clause break in each sentence and draw intonation arrows in each:

    a) I left early because I didn't like the film.
    b) It was past ten o'clock, so we had to go.
    c) Jim bought some cornflakes and a pie.
    d) The book was good at first, then boring.

3. Listen to four sentences and underline the key concept word or phrase in each one:

    a) I got the tube to work today.
    b) She left her brother at home.
    c) There are three biscuits left.
    d) I can't find the remote control.

4. Draw arrows to show standard intonation in each question:

    a) Do you like raw fish?
    b) We both enjoyed the gig, didn't we?
    c) This is the right bus, isn't it?
    d) What's the date today?

5. Listen to four questions. Match each question to an answer below:

    a) Perry did.
    b) Red.
    c) Yes, he did.
    d) Last week.

6. Write the tools in the intonation toolbox from the first letters:

    a) t _ of v _
    b) r _
    c) e _ e _
    d) p _ for e _
    e) p _
    f) s _
    g) v _

7. Listen to the sentence read with different moods. Match each version to a mood below:

    a) angry
    b) happy
    c) excited
    d) sad
    e) relieved
    f) apologetic

8. Complete the table to show what happens with four different moods. Write and read your own sentences out loud using the different moods:

tone of voice	pitch	extra emphasis on content words	volume	rhythm	speed	pausing (for effect)
nervous						
surprised						
tired						
disgusted						

9. Read each sentence out loud with neutral intonation, then in different moods (see *Role Plays – Mood Chart* on p.41). Which tools from the intonation toolbox did you use to make each mood?

    a) I've gone to the shops.
    b) He lived in Birmingham all his life.
    c) There are two sausages left in the oven.
    d) The garden needs watering.

10. i) Listen and match each short sound or word with a meaning below:

    a) I'm interested.
    b) I'm disappointed.
    c) I understand.
    d) It smells delicious.
    e) Stop! Come back!
    f) Thinking what to say.

    ii) Create a role play using only short sounds, intonation, and mime.

11. Discussion: How does your language compare to English when it comes to stress and intonation? Do you think there is too much of this in English? What short sounds do you use in your language, and what do they mean? List ones which are the same as in English. List ones which are different.

Role Plays – Mood Chart

I'm feeling...

nosey	bored	sad	cheerful
angry	happy	shocked	up
frightened	smug	apologetic	secretive
down	worried	so so	aggressive
guilty	ecstatic	paranoid	naughty
surprised	energetic	friendly	unwell
depressed	moody	determined	tired
giggly	upset	mischievous	disgusted
too hot	excited	cold	nervous
stupid	horrified	relieved	confused

21 English Sounds and Words where Intonation Changes the Meaning

There are some short sounds and words in English that have different meanings depending on the intonation. They are often more eloquent than many words! They are marked positive / negative / neutral (neither positive nor negative)

Short sounds and words (with translations):

sound / word:	rising ↗	flat →	falling ↘	rising-falling ↗↘
ah	1. I want to speak	2. An unexpected problem	3. I'm sorry / something's wrong	4. I understand at last
eh	5. What do you mean?	6. Listen / Come here	7. Don't do that	8. I'm consoling you
hey	9. Stop / Come back / Hi	10. Hi, I'm tired or feel down	11. I'm not happy about that	12. Wake up
oh	13. I'm interested	14. I'm annoyed	15. I'm disappointed	16. I understand at last
uh huh	17. Keep going – I'm listening	18. Still listening, but bored	19. I'm confirming sth	20. I get it / I understand
mmm	21. I'm interested	22. Pausing	23. I'm not sure about sth	24. It's delicious / It's good
no	25. I didn't know that	26. Refusal – no discussion	27. Standard negative reply	28. It's fine / I don't mind
right	29. I'm interested	30. My mind is elsewhere	31. I understand / before action	
sure	33. Are you sure about this?	34. Hurry up – I'm impatient	35. OK, I will do it	32. Sarcasm: I don't believe you
yeah	37. D'you want a fight?	38. I'm not listening	39. OK, I understand	36. Yes, I'm very happy to do it
yes	41. Tell me more / Can I help?	42. Please stop talking	43. I agree / I understand	40. Sarcasm: I don't agree
OK	45. Do you agree?	46. I'm frustrated / stop talking	47. I accept sth	44. I strongly agree / sarcasm
aah		49. I'm at the doctor's	50. I think sth is cute	48. I'm happy to agree
uh uh		52. Leave me alone (warning)	53. No / negative	51. I understand at last
wow		55. I can't believe it	56. I'm impressed	54. Strong negative answer
ooh			58. What a shame / pity!	57. It's incredible
yay			60. Ironic use – I'm not happy	59. Something good/interesting
yum yum	62. To a baby/pet: want to eat?			61. I'm surprised by good news
boo				63. It smells / tastes delicious
ugh			66. I hate that / I'm disgusted	64. I'm scaring you! (for fun)
ha ha		68. Sarcastic laughter	67. I'm very disgusted	65. It was a bad performance
				69. I'm laughing (maybe at you)

Other short sounds (with translations):

brrr		70. I feel cold / sth scary	
er		71. Pausing for thought	
ew			72. That's disgusting!
oof		73. What a shock / Disbelief	
ow			74. I'm hurt / it hurts
uh oh			75. Something has gone wrong
um	76. Pausing for thought		
whee			77. I'm enjoying sliding down
oops		78. I've had an accident	

Other common sounds with fixed meanings in English:

79. **clear throat**
Get attention, e.g. I'm about to speak / I'm nervous / Stop doing that

80. **draw in breath**
I'm worried that something bad is about to happen

81. **descending whistle**
I'm shocked / in awe of something

82. **lick lips**
I'm hungry / ready to eat

83. **singing** / 84. **humming**
I'm happy / in a good mood

85. **speak through gritted teeth**
I'm angry but trying not to show it – instead of shouting

86. **tutting (with tongue)**
I'm not happy, but too polite to complain

87. **melodious whistling**
I'm happy / in a good mood

88. **wolf whistle** / 89. **phwoar**
You look attractive (sexist)

90. **yawn**
I'm tired / bored / I want you to stop talking or go home

Unit 3.4 Past Simple and Past Continuous

3.4.1   **Past Simple** and **Past Continuous** are often used together because they happen in the same time: finished time in the past. For example:

- yesterday
- last... (e.g. last week / month / year)
- ...ago (e.g. two weeks / months / years ago)

Let's look at these tenses in more detail:

Tense:	Time:	Forms:	Auxiliary Verbs:	Example Sentences:
past simple	finished time in the past, (e.g. yesterday, last..., ...ago)	past tense infinitive (for negative and question forms)	did	+ I met my friend. - I did not meet my friend. / - I didn't meet my friend*. ? Did you meet your friend?
			was / were (if main verb is BE)	+ You were early. - You were not early. / - You weren't early*. ? Were you early?
past continuous	as above	ing form	was / were	+ I was watching TV. - I was not watching TV. / - I wasn't watching TV*. ? Were you watching TV?

* contraction (short form) is more informal

In short, we use past simple to talk about finished actions in the past – time which is finished, e.g.

- He got to work **at 8 o'clock yesterday morning**.

3.4.2   Past simple is the most commonly used tense in English. If you think about it, we use it all the time to talk about what happened in the past – to give news and tell stories.

For example:

- You get home from somewhere and tell your partner or friend a funny story about what happened that day, or previously in the past
- You go to the doctor's and tell them how you got a big bruise on your leg
- You read a newspaper article about something interesting that happened yesterday
- You read a novel in which almost every sentence uses past simple or past continuous and the past tense verb "said" appears many times on every page
- ...and so on!

3.4.3   Though not as common as past simple, we use past continuous when the action is continuous, i.e. for longer actions. Another difference is that in past continuous the action is often unfinished and interrupted:

past simple:	I brushed my teeth before going to bed.	*finished action*
past continuous:	I was brushing my teeth before going to bed when they all fell out!	*unfinished action*

We also use past continuous:

- *to set the scene* (see 3.4.4, below): I was making lunch when Bob got home.
- *to describe specific times in the past*: 'What were you doing at 1pm yesterday?' 'I was washing my car.'
- *to describe repeating actions in the past – with* always: Philip was always talking to his friends in class.

Past continuous is not usually found on its own in a sentence. We use it in the first clause (part) of the sentence, then often use a conjunction such as **and**, **but**, **because** (or **when** and **while**, see below), then another clause with a different tense – probably past simple. The following sentence would be odd, for example:

'I was reading a book.'   We have to ask, 'When?' or 'Which book?' etc.

In general, a sentence with past continuous on its own seems incomplete. An exception is when you describe repeating actions in the past with 'always' (see above), and also when you are **answering a question**, for example:

'What were you doing all morning?'   'I was reading a book.'

Note: it is not possible to use **state verbs** with past continuous, because they do not have ing forms. For example, we can say "I was enjoying the concert" because enjoy is an active verb, but not "I was liking the concert" because 'like' is a state verb.

3.4.4   We often put both tenses together in the same sentence, as in the second example above, using the conjunctions **when** and **while**:

I was walking to work when I met Bill.

We start with past continuous in the first clause of the sentence and then use when or while to connect to a past simple clause. If we use **when**, something happens **after** the past continuous clause; so past continuous is used to set the scene before a main action with past simple. If we use **while**, something happens **during** the past continuous clause:

when	I was eating an apple when the phone rang.	*p.s. action happens* **after** *p.c. action*
while	I was eating an apple while the phone rang.	*p.s. action happens* **during** *p.c. action*

3.4.5   This table can help us to understand the differences between these two common tenses:

	Past Simple	Past Continuous
Example:	I ate breakfast yesterday.	I was eating breakfast yesterday.
Time:	past (finished time)	past (finished time)
Forms:	past tense infinitive (for questions and negatives) -ed (regular verbs) / if irregular, learn the form(s)	ing form (present participle)
Auxiliary Verbs:	did / did not (didn't) if main verb is BE, use was, were	was / was not (wasn't) were / were not (weren't)
Typical Times:	yesterday / last… / …ago	yesterday / last… / …ago when / while an action is in progress before or during a past simple action
Uses:	finished actions in the past to tell stories / news second conditional (unreal future)	interrupted actions in the past to set the scene in the past specific times in the past, e.g. at 2 o'clock repetition with always

3.4.6   As you can see from the information above, in past simple we have to remember to use did + infinitive form to make negative and question forms. This is not really logical and students often forget to do this extra thing – it's just one more thing to remember! It would be far more logical if we could say:

positive	He went to the shop yesterday.	✓
negative	He no went to the shop yesterday.	X
question form	He went to the shop yesterday? (with rising intonation)	X

Of course, this is the way that many students make negative and question forms in past simple, perhaps because it is more logical or closer to their first language. However, we must remember to take that extra step and use **did + infinitive form**.

3.4.7   In past simple we need to use **past tense form**. Past tense form is similar to **past participle form** (used for **present perfect**) because with both forms it is necessary to know about **irregular verbs**. We add -ed to a regular verb to make both past tense and past participle forms, but since irregular verbs are all different (they are *irregular!*) we have no choice but to learn the different forms. There are thousands of regular verbs in English, with -ed endings, and only a few hundred common irregular verbs. The problem is that irregular verbs occur very frequently, so it is necessary to learn the different past tense and past participle forms. That is why you will often see a chart of irregular verbs on the classroom wall at a language school. There is no getting away from irregular verb endings – you just have to learn them, if you want to be correct using past simple.

3.4.8   On the next two pages you can see how the most common verbs in English – BE, DO, HAVE, and GO – look in past simple and past continuous tenses. Try to learn these important verb tables.

The Most Important Verbs in English – Past Simple

BE

	Positive:	Negative:	Question:
I	was	was not / wasn't	Was I?
you	were	were not / weren't	Were you?
he	was	was not / wasn't	Was he?
she	was	was not / wasn't	Was she?
it	was	was not / wasn't	Was it?
we	were	were not / weren't	Were we?
they	were	were not / weren't	Were they?

DO

	Positive:	Negative:	Question:
I	did	did not / didn't	Did I?
you	did	did not / didn't	Did you?
he	did	did not / didn't	Did he?
she	did	did not / didn't	Did she?
it	did	did not / didn't	Did it?
we	did	did not / didn't	Did we?
they	did	did not / didn't	Did they?

HAVE

	Positive:	Negative*:	Question:
I	had	had not / did not have	Had I? / Did I have?
you	had	had not / did not have	Had you? / Did you have?
he	had	had not / did not have	Had he? / Did he have?
she	had	had not / did not have	Had she? / Did she have?
it	had	had not / did not have	Had it? / Did it have?
we	had	had not / did not have	Had we? / Did we have?
they	had	had not / did not have	Had they? / Did they have?

GO

	Positive:	Negative:	Question:
I	went	did not go / didn't go	Did I go?
you	went	did not go / didn't go	Did you go?
he	went	did not go / didn't go	Did he go?
she	went	did not go / didn't go	Did she go?
it	went	did not go / didn't go	Did it go?
we	went	did not go / didn't go	Did we go?
they	went	did not go / didn't go	Did they go?

*contractions are possible, e.g. I had not = I hadn't; she did not have = she didn't have, etc.

The Most Important Verbs in English – Past Continuous

BE

	Positive:	Negative:	Question:
I	was being	was not being / wasn't being	Was I being?
you	were being	were not being / weren't being	Were you being?
he	was being	was not being / wasn't being	Was he being?
she	was being	was not being / wasn't being	Was she being?
it	was being	was not being / wasn't being	Was it being?
we	were being	were not being / weren't being	Were we being?
they	were being	were not being / weren't being	Were they being?

DO

	Positive:	Negative:	Question:
I	was doing	was not doing / wasn't doing	Was I doing?
you	were doing	were not doing / weren't doing	Were you doing?
he	was doing	was not doing / wasn't doing	Was he doing?
she	was doing	was not doing / wasn't doing	Was she doing?
it	was doing	was not doing / wasn't doing	Was it doing?
we	were doing	were not doing / weren't doing	Were we doing?
they	were doing	were not doing / weren't doing	Were they doing?

HAVE

	Positive:	Negative:	Question:
I	was having	was not having / wasn't having	Was I having?
you	were having	were not having / weren't having	Were you having?
he	was having	was not having / wasn't having	Was he having?
she	was having	was not having / wasn't having	Was she having?
it	was having	was not having / wasn't having	Was it having?
we	were having	were not having / weren't having	Were we having?
they	were having	were not having / weren't having	Were they having?

GO

	Positive:	Negative:	Question:
I	was going	was not going / wasn't going	Was I going?
you	were going	were not going / weren't going	Were you going?
he	was going	was not going / wasn't going	Was he going?
she	was going	was not going / wasn't going	Was she going?
it	was going	was not going / wasn't going	Was it going?
we	were going	were not going / weren't going	Were we going?
they	were going	were not going / weren't going	Were they going?

Exercises

Ex. 3.4.1   **Writing** Complete the sentences below using one of these past tense verbs:

went   ate   watched   rained   came   enjoyed   had   drank   heard   walked

1. Last week I _____ to London for the weekend.
2. I _____ you talking about my friend yesterday.
3. Last night I _____ a film about space travel.
4. I missed the bus so I _____ home.
5. I'm not here on my own. My friend _____ with me.
6. We _____ the concert.
7. It _____ this morning so I didn't go out.
8. I _____ two glasses of water before going to bed.
9. I _____ some cereal and toast for my breakfast.
10. I went to the shop to see if they _____ any postcards.

Ex. 3.4.2   **Writing** Complete the sentences below using one of these past tense verbs:

went   laughed   made   thought   left   bought   finished   tried   wanted   cooked

1. I _____ a really nice meal for my mum's birthday.
2. My brother _____ to come too, but he wasn't allowed.
3. We all _____ when Tina fell off her chair!
4. I think that we were _____ for each other!
5. Kim and Charlotte _____ the party at 1.40am.
6. He _____ to call you but couldn't get through.
7. I _____ about driving to the coast for the weekend.
8. Tessa _____ her wedding dress last Monday.
9. I went home after the concert _____.
10. My friends all _____ to see the new exhibition in town.

Ex. 3.4.3   **Writing** Complete the verb tables using **past simple** (positive):

to be:
I _____
You _____
He _____
She _____
It _____
We _____
They _____

to have:
I _____
You _____
He _____
She _____
It _____
We _____
They _____

to do:
I _____
You _____
He _____
She _____
It _____
We _____
They _____

to go:
I _____
You _____
He _____
She _____
It _____
We _____
They _____

Ex. 3.4.4   **Writing** Complete the verb tables using **past continuous** (positive):

to be:
I _____
You _____
He _____
She _____
It _____
We _____
They _____

to have:
I _____
You _____
He _____
She _____
It _____
We _____
They _____

to do:
I _____
You _____
He _____
She _____
It _____
We _____
They _____

to go:
I _____
You _____
He _____
She _____
It _____
We _____
They _____

Ex. 3.4.5   **Writing** Rearrange the words in each sentence to make a question in **past simple**. Don't forget to put a capital letter at the start of each sentence and a question mark at the end:

1. company you which did recommend taxi
2. last watch did film you night that
3. did you learning when English start
4. results your about you ask did
5. call your morning why this you boss did
6. did Tina say to what you
7. on parcel arrive time your did
8. go how your did exam
9. you did party who to invite your
10. the rest did where go cheesecake of the

Ex. 3.4.6   **Writing** Rearrange the words in each sentence to make a question in **past continuous** tense. Don't forget to put a capital letter at the start of each sentence and a question mark at the end:

1. you the as leaving arrived was train just
2. you phone when kitchen going the were rang the into
3. most night posts of were reading on the you Twitter funny
4. you Tim's of meal my to were thinking mother birthday inviting
5. in yesterday annoying buzzing the was an manner bee around
6. you up about were in-jokes always Kevin making
7. uncle the running was when your began earthquake bath a
8. when their salad to the refusing grandma children eat were arrived
9. heading when exploded for it the was straight earth meteorite
10. Lena's a to former son husband was meet marriage going his from

Ex. 3.4.7 **Writing** Write 10 sentences using this model:

past continuous   +   conjunction   +   past simple

1. I was _____ when _____
2. You were _____ while _____
3. He was _____ but _____
4. She was _____ because _____
5. It was _____ and _____
6. We were _____ or _____
7. They were _____ when _____
8. I was _____ while _____
9. You were _____ but _____
10. We were _____ because _____

Ex. 3.4.8 **Writing** a) Write about what you were doing yesterday at the following times. Use past continuous and try to use a different verb for each sentence. For example:

At 4 pm I was reading a book.

1. At 6.30 am _____
2. At 7.45 am _____
3. At 8.25 am _____
4. At 9.05 am _____
5. At 10.40 am _____
6. At 11.15 am _____
7. At 12.50 pm _____
8. At 2 pm _____
9. At 3.23 pm _____
10. At 4 pm _____
11. At 5.35 pm _____
12. At 6.48 pm _____
13. At 7.55 pm _____
14. At 9.05 pm _____
15. At 11 pm _____

b) Ask your partner about what they were doing yesterday and complete the sentences again. Or think of a famous person and imagine what they were doing!

Ex. 3.4.9 **Writing** Complete each sentence using either **yesterday** or **tomorrow**:

1. I went to the cinema _____.
2. I'm playing golf _____.
3. We had an early lunch _____.
4. Her sister is going into hospital _____.
5. What time are you getting up _____?
6. I'm taking the car to the garage first thing _____.
7. My brother moved house _____.
8. Did you see that new music shop in town _____?
9. I met Lisa and Isabella for a coffee _____.
10. He's visiting his friend _____ afternoon.
11. There was a lot of noise outside _____.
12. We're going swimming _____ morning.
13. Are you coming round _____ evening?
14. He wasn't at work _____ afternoon because he went to hospital for an appointment.
15. John was in Birmingham all day _____ for a meeting.
16. I gave them some homework _____.

Elementary English Course

17. I'm not going on holiday until _____.
18. I missed the last bus _____, so I had to walk home.
19. It was cold _____, wasn't it?
20. Sally is getting her exam results _____.
21. We packed our suitcases _____ evening.
22. Is he still cooking lunch for his girlfriend and her family _____?
23. Bob and Janet are coming round for a game of cards _____ night.
24. We're flying to Spain _____ afternoon.
25. He's playing football for a couple of hours _____ morning.
26. I saw your friend Ian in Sainsbury's _____.
27. I'm doing all my ironing _____.
28. We both bought the same pair of shoes _____.
29. Is he going to tell you about the course _____, or later on today?
30. Jen swam forty lengths of the pool _____.

Ex. 3.4.10   **Writing** Complete the table from memory, then check your answers:

	Past Simple	Past Continuous
Example: *Time:*		
Forms:		
Auxiliary Verbs:		
Typical Times:		
Uses:		

Unit 3.5 Common Regular and Irregular Verbs

3.5.1   Look at the list of the 40 most common verbs in English on p.57. It is a really good idea to set yourself the goal of learning them, along with all five forms. In the last column on the right we can see whether each verb is **regular** or **irregular**. Every verb in English is either regular or irregular. The difference is in the past tense and past participle forms. If the verb is regular, these two forms end with 'ed', for example:

  I look   I look**ed**   I have look**ed**

  If the verb is irregular, the endings vary, for example:

  I give   **I gave**   I have **given**

3.5.2   There are thousands of regular verbs in English compared with a few hundred irregular verbs. (See the list of 40 common regular verbs on p.58.) The problem for students is that these regular verbs are very common, describing many everyday actions and states, like: be, have, do, say, go, get, make, put, etc. Note that in the list of the 40 most common verbs in English <u>27 of the verbs are irregular!</u> If we make new verbs, we generally make them regular. Nobody wants to create new irregular verbs that we have to learn. For example:

  He spams us   He spamm**ed** us   He has spamm**ed** us
  (sends spam)

  She chillaxes   She chillax**ed**   She has chillax**ed**
  (a cross between chill out and relax)

  This goes for other newly-coined verbs too, like: email / emailed; tweet / tweeted; unfriend / unfriended; photobomb / photobombed; facepalm / facepalmed; snapchat / snapchatted; glamp / glamped, etc. One exception is the verb to text:

  Is it: I texted John last night.   Or,   I text John last night?

  The latter is much easier to pronounce, and some people treat 'text' as an irregular verb, while others say that it is regular, with -ed. There is no authority giving rules to the English language, so both uses can be correct. Other verbs can be both regular and irregular at the same time too, e.g.

  <u>regular:</u>   <u>irregular:</u>
  burned   burnt
  dreamed   dreamt
  learned   learnt

  ...and so on. You can use either form, but the -ed ending is accepted as the modern form.

3.5.3   In general, it would be better for learners of English if all English verbs could be regular! If English could be reformed so that learners just added -ed to every verb to make past tense and past participle forms, it would remove a big headache from the learning process. For example we could see the following new regular verbs:

  doed   goed   maked
  sayed   getted   knowed

...and so on. I feel sure that the language would survive such a change! In fact, when English native speaker children begin to write their own sentences and stories at primary school they often naturally write irregular verbs as regular, with -ed endings, for example:

| I thinked... | *instead of* | I thought... |
| I telled her... | *instead of* | I told her... |

Children learning English grammar often sense a logical rule – past tense of verbs end in -ed – only for their teacher to dash their hopes:

Teacher: No, that's wrong. It should be 'thought'.

Child: But why?

Teacher: It's just like that.   *or, more helpful:*   Because 'think' is an irregular verb...

Child: But why?

Teacher: Er... [long pause] It just *is*, OK?

3.5.4 In terms of spelling, we usually add -ed to regular verbs to make the past tense and past participle forms:

| want | + ed | = | wanted |
| work | + ed | = | worked |

However, if a verb ends with 'e' we add only 'd':

| change | + d | = | changed |
| love | + d | = | loved |

Sometimes we have to double the final consonant before adding -ed:

| beg | + g + ed | = | begged |
| rob | + b + ed | = | robbed |

Sometimes we have to delete the 'y' at the end of an infinitive verb and add 'ied':

| fry | - y + ied | = | fried |
| try | - y + ied | = | tried |

3.5.5 If a verb is irregular you just have to learn the different forms. (See the list of 40 common irregular verbs on p.59.) It is impossible to predict the forms of irregular verbs and there is no choice but to learn them. You need to get familiar with them, study them, test yourself, correct yourself, study them again, and continue the process until you know them by heart. A small number of irregular verbs have three forms the same, e.g. let, put, hit, bet, bid, set, cut, shut, cut, spread, and quit:

<u>infinitive:</u>   <u>past tense:</u>   <u>past participle:</u>
I let   every day   I let   yesterday   I have let   today
I put   I put   I have put

Some irregular verbs have two forms the same, e.g.:

infinitive:	past tense:	past participle:
I feel	I felt	I have felt
I make	I made	I have made

While the rest have three forms different, e.g.:

infinitive:	past tense:	past participle:
I give	I gave	I have given
I see	I saw	I have seen

3.5.6 The -ed ending of regular verbs is pronounced in three different ways, depending on the final sound of the infinitive verb. See p.67 to learn more about this issue. On p.68 there is a list of 200 common regular verbs in English, ordered by final sound.

Exercises

Ex. 3.5.1 **Writing** Complete the table on p.60.

Ex. 3.5.2 **Writing** Regular verbs – complete the gaps in the table on p.61.

Ex. 3.5.3 **Writing** Irregular verbs – complete the gaps in the table on p.62.

Ex. 3.5.4 **Writing** Write each verb in the correct box below:

want	take	use	seem	arrive	go	need	be
know	try	help	have	get	ask	call	think
play	make	say	work	do	clean	run	sing

regular verbs:	irregular verbs:

Elementary English Course

The 40 Most Common Verbs in English (in order)

Each English verb has five forms. We use different forms to make different tenses:

#	infinitive	s form	past tense	past participle	ing form	regular or irregular
1	be	am, are, is	was, were	been	being	I
2	have	has	had	had	having	I
3	do	does	did	done	doing	I
4	say	says	said	said	saying	I
5	go	goes	went	been / gone	going	I
6	get	gets	got	got	getting	I
7	make	makes	made	made	making	I
8	know	knows	knew	known	knowing	I
9	think	thinks	thought	thought	thinking	I
10	take	takes	took	taken	taking	I
11	see	sees	saw	seen	seeing	I
12	come	comes	came	come	coming	I
13	want	wants	wanted	wanted	wanting	R
14	use	uses	used	used	using	R
15	find	finds	found	found	finding	I
16	give	gives	gave	given	giving	I
17	tell	tells	told	told	telling	I
18	work	works	worked	worked	working	R
19	call	calls	called	called	calling	R
20	try	tries	tried	tried	trying	R
21	ask	asks	asked	asked	asking	R
22	need	needs	needed	needed	needing	R
23	feel	feels	felt	felt	feeling	I
24	become	becomes	became	become	becoming	I
25	leave	leaves	left	left	leaving	I
26	put	puts	put	put	putting	I
27	mean	means	meant	meant	meaning	I
28	keep	keeps	kept	kept	keeping	I
29	let	lets	let	let	letting	I
30	begin	begins	began	begun	beginning	I
31	seem	seems	seemed	seemed	seeming	R
32	help	helps	helped	helped	helping	R
33	show	shows	showed	shown	showing	I
34	hear	hears	heard	heard	hearing	I
35	play	plays	played	played	playing	R
36	run	runs	ran	run	running	I
37	move	moves	moved	moved	moving	R
38	live	lives	lived	lived	living	R
39	believe	believes	believed	believed	believing	R
40	bring	brings	brought	brought	bringing	I

Elementary English Course

Learn 40 Common Regular Verbs in English

infinitive:	s form:	past tense:	past participle:	ing form:
add	adds	added	added	adding
chat	chats	chatted	chatted	chatting
need	needs	needed	needed	needing
start	starts	started	started	starting
text	texts	texted	texted	texting
visit	visits	visited	visited	visiting
wait	waits	waited	waited	waiting
want	wants	wanted	wanted	wanting

If the verb ends with t or d sound, pronounce uhd

allow	allows	allowed	allowed	allowing
play	plays	played	played	playing
share	shares	shared	shared	sharing

If the verb ends with a vowel sound, pronounce d

arrive	arrives	arrived	arrived	arriving
call	calls	called	called	calling
change	changes	changed	changed	changing
clean	cleans	cleaned	cleaned	cleaning
close	closes	closed	closed	closing
earn	earns	earned	earned	earning
learn	learns	learned	learned	learning
listen	listens	listened	listened	listening
live	lives	lived	lived	living
love	loves	loved	loved	loving
open	opens	opened	opened	opening
pull	pulls	pulled	pulled	pulling
receive	receives	received	received	receiving
use	uses	used	used	using

*If the verb ends with a **voiced** consonant sound, pronounce d*

finish	finishes	finished	finished	finishing
help	helps	helped	helped	helping
kiss	kisses	kissed	kissed	kissing
laugh	laughs	laughed	laughed	laughing
like	likes	liked	liked	liking
look	looks	looked	looked	looking
push	pushes	pushed	pushed	pushing
stop	stops	stopped	stopped	stopping
talk	talks	talked	talked	talking
thank	thanks	thanked	thanked	thanking
touch	touches	touched	touched	touching
walk	walks	walked	walked	walking
wash	washes	washed	washed	washing
watch	watches	watched	watched	watching
work	works	worked	worked	working

*If the verb ends with an **unvoiced** consonant sound, pronounce t*

Elementary English Course

Learn 40 Common Irregular Verbs in English

	infinitive:	s form:	past tense:	past participle:	ing form:
1.	be	am, is, are	was, were	been	being
2.	begin	begins	began	begun	beginning
3.	break	breaks	broke	broken	breaking
4.	bring	brings	brought	brought	bringing
5.	buy	buys	bought	bought	buying
6.	cost	costs	cost	cost	costing
7.	do	does	did	done	doing
8.	drive	drives	drove	driven	driving
9.	fall	falls	fell	fallen	falling
10.	feel	feels	felt	felt	feeling
11.	find	finds	found	found	finding
12.	get	gets	got	got	getting
13.	give	gives	gave	given	giving
14.	go	goes	went	been / gone	going
15.	grow	grows	grew	grown	growing
16.	have	has	had	had	having
17.	hear	hears	heard	heard	hearing
18.	hold	holds	held	held	holding
19.	keep	keeps	kept	kept	keeping
20.	know	knows	knew	known	knowing
21.	lead	leads	led	led	leading
22.	leave	leaves	left	left	leaving
23.	lose	loses	lost	lost	losing
24.	make	makes	made	made	making
25.	mean	means	meant	meant	meaning
26.	meet	meets	met	met	meeting
27.	put	puts	put	put	putting
28.	read	reads	read	read	reading
29.	say	says	said	said	saying
30.	see	sees	saw	seen	seeing
31.	show	shows	showed	shown	showing
32.	sit	sits	sat	sat	sitting
33.	speak	speaks	spoke	spoken	speaking
34.	spend	spends	spent	spent	spending
35.	stand	stands	stood	stood	standing
36.	take	takes	took	taken	taking
37.	tell	tells	told	told	telling
38.	think	thinks	thought	thought	thinking
39.	win	wins	won	won	winning
40.	write	writes	wrote	written	writing

Elementary English Course

The 40 Most Common Verbs in English (in order) – Gap-Fill

Each English verb has five forms. We use different forms to make different tenses:

#	infinitive	s form	past tense	past participle	ing form	regular or irregular
1	be					
2	have					
3	do					
4	say					
5	go					
6	get					
7	make					
8	know					
9	think					
10	take					
11	see					
12	come					
13	want					
14	use					
15	find					
16	give					
17	tell					
18	work					
19	call					
20	try					
21	ask					
22	need					
23	feel					
24	become					
25	leave					
26	put					
27	mean					
28	keep					
29	let					
30	begin					
31	seem					
32	help					
33	show					
34	hear					
35	play					
36	run					
37	move					
38	live					
39	believe					
40	bring					

Elementary English Course

Learn 40 Common Regular Verbs in English – Practice

infinitive:	s form:	past tense:	past participle:	ing form:
add	1. _____	added	added	adding
chat	chats	2. _____	chatted	chatting
need	needs	needed	3. _____	needing
start	starts	started	started	4. _____
text	5. _____	texted	texted	texting
visit	visits	6. _____	visited	visiting
wait	waits	waited	7. _____	waiting
want	wants	wanted	wanted	8. _____

If the verb ends with t or d sound, pronounce uhd

allow	9. _____	allowed	allowed	allowing
play	plays	10. _____	played	playing
share	shares	shared	11. _____	sharing

If the verb ends with a vowel sound, pronounce d

arrive	arrives	arrived	arrived	12. _____
call	13. _____	called	called	calling
change	changes	14. _____	changed	changing
clean	cleans	cleaned	15. _____	cleaning
close	closes	closed	closed	16. _____
earn	17. _____	earned	earned	earning
learn	learns	18. _____	learned	learning
listen	listens	listened	19. _____	listening
live	lives	lived	lived	20. _____
love	21. _____	loved	loved	loving
open	opens	22. _____	opened	opening
pull	pulls	pulled	23. _____	pulling
receive	receives	received	received	24. _____
use	25. _____	used	used	using

*If the verb ends with a **voiced** consonant sound, pronounce d*

finish	finishes	26. _____	finished	finishing
help	helps	helped	27. _____	helping
kiss	kisses	kissed	kissed	28. _____
laugh	29. _____	laughed	laughed	laughing
like	likes	30. _____	liked	liking
look	looks	looked	31. _____	looking
push	pushes	pushed	pushed	32. _____
stop	33. _____	stopped	stopped	stopping
talk	talks	34. _____	talked	talking
thank	thanks	thanked	35. _____	thanking
touch	touches	touched	touched	36. _____
walk	37. _____	walked	walked	walking
wash	washes	38. _____	washed	washing
watch	watches	watched	39. _____	watching
work	works	worked	worked	40. _____

*If the verb ends with an **unvoiced** consonant sound, pronounce t*

Elementary English Course

Learn 40 Common Irregular Verbs in English – Practice

	infinitive:	s form:	past tense:	past participle:	ing form:
1.	be	_____	was, were	been	being
2.	begin	begins	_____	begun	beginning
3.	break	breaks	broke	_____	breaking
4.	bring	brings	brought	brought	_____
5.	buy	_____	bought	bought	buying
6.	cost	costs	_____	cost	costing
7.	do	does	did	_____	doing
8.	drive	drives	drove	driven	_____
9.	fall	_____	fell	fallen	falling
10.	feel	feels	_____	felt	feeling
11.	find	finds	found	_____	finding
12.	get	gets	got	got	_____
13.	give	_____	gave	given	giving
14.	go	goes	_____	been / gone	going
15.	grow	grows	grew	_____	growing
16.	have	has	had	had	_____
17.	hear	_____	heard	heard	hearing
18.	hold	holds	_____	held	holding
19.	keep	keeps	kept	_____	keeping
20.	know	knows	knew	known	_____
21.	lead	_____	led	led	leading
22.	leave	leaves	_____	left	leaving
23.	lose	loses	lost	_____	losing
24.	make	makes	made	made	_____
25.	mean	_____	meant	meant	meaning
26.	meet	meets	_____	met	meeting
27.	put	puts	put	_____	putting
28.	read	reads	read	read	_____
29.	say	_____	said	said	saying
30.	see	sees	_____	seen	seeing
31.	show	shows	showed	_____	showing
32.	sit	sits	sat	sat	_____
33.	speak	_____	spoke	spoken	speaking
34.	spend	spends	_____	spent	spending
35.	stand	stands	stood	_____	standing
36.	take	takes	took	taken	_____
37.	tell	_____	told	told	telling
38.	think	thinks	_____	thought	thinking
39.	win	wins	won	_____	winning
40.	write	writes	wrote	written	_____

Ex. 3.5.5   **Reading** Complete each sentence by adding the **best** form of the verb:

1. I (been/went/gone) _____ shopping yesterday.
2. He hasn't (bought/bring/brought) _____ his passport.
3. Emily (choose/chosed/chose) _____ a light blue carpet for her living room.
4. Have you (get/got/getted) _____ your train ticket?
5. James (drove/drive/driven) _____ a long way to visit his girlfriend, but she was out.
6. I have (grow/growed/grown) _____ two big tomato plants.
7. Don (put/putted/puts) _____ his bag on the table and went upstairs.
8. I (thinked/thunk/thought) _____ I (knew/new/known) _____ you from somewhere.
9. We (leaved/left/leaving) _____ on Monday night at about eight o'clock.
10. Sarah has (swim/swam/swum) _____ for her country in the Olympics.
11. Lenny (wore/weared/wearing) _____ a new suit and tie to work.
12. The whole kitchen (stink/stank/stinked) _____ of garlic and onions!
13. Darling, you have (stole/stolen/stealed) _____ my heart!
14. Maggie (taken/took/taked) _____ a pen out of her bag and wrote a quick note to her husband.
15. Ludwig van Beethoven (wrote/written/writed) _____ some fantastic symphonies.

Ex. 3.5.6   **Reading** Write the sentences again, changing each underlined verb from the present simple to the past simple tense:

1. I wake up at 6.50am when I hear the alarm clock.
2. I jump out of bed and switch it off before it wakes up all the neighbours.
3. I switch on the light and the heater, because it's cold in my room.
4. I use the bathroom; then look for a clean shirt to wear.
5. I go into the kitchen and put the kettle on.
6. I get dressed and brush my hair.
7. I have a shave and then pack my bag ready for work.
8. The kettle boils so I make a cup of tea; then I watch TV for a few minutes.
9. I open all the curtains in my house and pick up my sandwiches from the fridge.
10. I put on my shoes and coat; then check that I haven't forgotten anything.
11. I leave on the light in the hall because I know it will be dark when I get home.
12. I unlock and open the front door; then I go outside.
13. I lock the front door and walk a few metres to my car.
14. I get into the car and turn the key in the ignition.
15. I put on a tape and turn up the volume.
16. I look in my mirrors, then reverse up the drive and onto the road.
17. I drive for five miles until I reach a traffic-jam.
18. I sit in the traffic-jam for twenty minutes; I drive forward slowly, a few metres at a time.
19. I change the tape in my car stereo, and tap my fingers on the steering wheel.
20. I put on the radio and listen to the news, followed by the weather forecast.
21. The radio plays one of my favourite songs, so I sing along loudly.
22. I turn right into the road where I always leave my car. I park and turn off the engine.
23. I get out and shut the door. I lock my car door and then walk for about twenty minutes.
24. I buy a newspaper and a sandwich at the newsagent; then I head for work.
25. As I enter the building I say "Hi" to the people I work with.
26. I get to my desk at about 8.50 am and put down my bag.
27. I'm ready for another cup of tea and to ~~have a long nap~~ start the day!

Ex. 3.5.7   **Writing** Translate 20 common irregular verbs **from** Clear Alphabet (see Unit 1.6):

1. Bee _____
2. Reed _____
3. Hiy _____
4. See _____
5. Bai _____
6. Breik _____
7. Eet _____
8. Rait _____
9. Sleep _____
10. Meet _____
11. Faind _____
12. Bring _____
13. Greu _____
14. Ttingk _____
15. Neu _____
16. bi Kum _____
17. Draiv _____
18. f Get _____
19. Leev _____
20. Tel _____

Ex. 3.5.8   **Writing** Translate 20 common irregular verbs **into** Clear Alphabet:

1. make _____
2. build _____
3. lose _____
4. take _____
5. drink _____
6. let _____
7. have _____
8. can _____
9. do _____
10. catch _____
11. ring _____
12. get _____
13. feel _____
14. go _____
15. put _____
16. pay _____
17. wear _____
18. send _____
19. understand _____
20. fly _____

Ex. 3.5.9   **Reading** Complete each gap with an irregular verb in past simple. Choose from:

> be, break, buy, come, drive, eat, feel, find, get, give, go, have, hear, hold, know, let, lose, make, put, read, ring, run, say, sleep, take, think, tell, write

Note: you will need to use some verbs more than once.

Dear Ethel

I'm writing to tell you about something that happened yesterday. I 1)_____ up at the usual time – about 10 am – 2)_____ a shower and 3)_____ breakfast. I 4)_____ a big bowl of cereal and some toast and watched TV for a while. Then I 5)_____ into the kitchen where I 6)_____ a funny noise. I 7)_____ it 8)_____ from behind the cooker. I 9)_____ my tool box and moved the cooker out of the way.

The noise 10)_____ louder but I couldn't see anything. I 11)_____ my uncle to ask his advice. He 12)_____ that he 13)_____ it could be a gas leak. When I 14)_____ this I just panicked! I 15)_____ the phone down, 16)_____ outside, 17)_____ in my car and 18)_____ to the local police station. I 19)_____ them about my gas leak but the constable 20)_____ his patience with me. He 21)_____ that I should have phoned the gas company. He 22)_____ his report, then 23)_____ the gas company for me.

Then I remembered that my house doesn't have gas – only electricity! I 24)_____ really stupid and 25)_____ that the constable would be angry with me for wasting his time, so I 26)_____ out of the police station while he 27)_____ still on the phone. I 28)_____ home to try to find out what the noise 29)_____. On the way I 30)_____ a newspaper and I 31)_____ about an escaped llama that 32)_____ out of the city safari park last Wednesday.

When I 33)_____ home I 34)_____ my key in the door, turned it, 35)_____ inside and straight away 36)_____ that funny noise again. I 37)_____ my breath and opened the door slowly. Guess what? I 38)_____ the llama hiding in my cupboard! I 39)_____ him stay and he 40)_____ in my garden last night. The snoring 41)_____ so loud! This morning I 42)_____ him back to the safari park. They 43)_____ really pleased to see him again and 44)_____ me a reward of £50!

Hope you are well. Write soon and let me know how you are. Your friend,

Alan

Ex. 3.5.10 **Reading** a) Read the story below. All of the irregular verbs in **past tense** have the wrong ending – a regular -ed ending! Underline each one. b) Write the story again, using the correct past tense form of each irregular verb. c) Underline the regular verbs in **past tense** form:

A few days ago Michael Morrison heared a really good programme about yaks on the radio. He remembered that he once readed a very interesting book about yaks, and he decided to buy a copy and read it again. The next day he waked up early, haved a shower, getted dressed, runned downstairs, haved breakfast, then phoned his friend Mandy Minton, who beed a zoologist, but unfortunately she didn't know about the book. Michael putted on his coat and goed outside. He drived to the library and asked the assistant if they haved a copy of "Yaks of the World – Illustrated Edition". The assistant thinked for a moment and spended a few minutes checking the records on his computer, but nothing comed up.

Michael leaved the library and walked into town. He stopped at the huge bookstore on Crompton Street and goed in. He browsed the books, but could not find "Yaks of the World" anywhere – illustrated or not. A bookseller sayed that there *beed* a book called "Just Yaks", but Michael did not want it. A passing vegan telled Michael to try a specialist bookseller on Marriott Street – a place where they selled unusual books. Michael thanked the lady and payed for a copy of "Bridge Repair Weekly" magazine. At the specialist bookstore on Marriott Street Michael feeled sure that he would find the book he wanted, but after talking with a very quiet man in a long cardigan, Michael understanded that they didn't have any books about yaks – or indeed any other kind of long-haired animal. He exited the shop sadly and drived home.

He maked a quick sandwich and watched an excellent online video about clever llamas on YouTube. Then he haved a bright idea: "I haven't looked online for the book yet!" He spended the next few hours searching for the book in online bookstores, auction sites, and forums – but without any luck. There beed no such book as: "Yaks of the World – Illustrated Edition" "Maybe I dreamed it," he sighed to himself and goed to bed, where he doed in fact dream about finding the book. In his dream he seed it at the bottom of his wardrobe, underneath a pile of socks. When he waked up he looked in his wardrobe, but there beed not any books there. Only the socks.

A fews days later, Michael sitted down at his computer and begined to write the first chapter of "Yaks of the World – Illustrated Edition". After fourteen years of hard work – including many trips to the zoo – it beed finally ready to publish and it becomed a number one bestseller – among zoologists.

Elementary English Course

How to Pronounce the Past -ed Form of Regular Verbs

The past forms (2nd and 3rd forms) of all regular verbs in English end in "-ed". Sometimes "-ed" is pronounced uhd, sometimes d, and sometimes t. It depends on the **sound** (not the spelling) at the end of the infinitive form of the verb:

1. If the verb ends with a t sound, "-ed" is pronounced as an extra syllable uhd
e.g. "accepted" is pronounced uh Kse ptd   All of these verbs (and more) follow this pattern:

> accept, admit, alienate, attempt, attract, chat, cheat, communicate, complete, correct, create, debate, distract, doubt, exist, experiment, fascinate, fit, hate, hunt, invent, invite, last, paint, point, post, print, protect, start, suggest, tempt, test, text, trust, visit, wait, want, waste

2. If the verb ends with a d sound, "-ed" is pronounced as an extra syllable uhd
e.g. "wanted" is pronounced Won td   All of these verbs (and more) follow this pattern:

> add, applaud, ascend, attend, avoid, decide, descend, end, explode, extend, fade, fold, forward, guard, include, intend, load, mend, need, recommend, record, succeed, suspend, trade

3. If the verb ends with a vowel sound – *any* vowel sound – "-ed" is pronounced as d
e.g. "admired" is pronounced uh Dmaiyd   All of these verbs (and more) follow this pattern:

> admire, agree, allow, annoy, appear, bother, care, continue, deliver, employ, empty, enjoy, enter, fry, glue, lie, matter, offer, order, owe, play, prefer, reply, share, spare, try, weigh, worry

4. If the verb ends with a *voiced* consonant sound "-ed" is pronounced as d. Voiced consonant sounds are: b, g, v, th, r, w, y, m, n, ng, l, z, zz, j
e.g. "cleaned" is pronounced Kleend   All of these verbs (and more) follow this pattern:

> clean, complain, earn, explain, happen, imagine, join, learn, listen, loan, open, own, phone, rain, return, stain, train, apologise, close, erase, praise, realise, suppose, surprise, use, charm, climb, dream, form, perform, seem, achieve, arrive, behave, improve, live, love, move, preserve, boil, call, fill, handle, pull, travel, arrange, challenge, change, manage, bathe, beg, belong, rob

5. If the verb ends with an *unvoiced* consonant sound "-ed" is pronounced as t. Unvoiced consonant sounds are: tt, p, k, s, sh, ch, h, f, hh
e.g. "baked" is pronounced Beikt   All of these verbs (and more) follow this pattern:

> bake, book, check, kick, knock, like, look, talk, thank, walk, work, fax, fix, guess, kiss, pass, promise, pronounce, match, reach, touch, watch, finish, push, rush, wash, hope, stop, laugh

Final advice: the main thing is to avoid saying uhd when it is not necessary. The d and t sounds actually sound very similar, so don't worry if you get them mixed up sometimes. To sum up – learn the five rules on this page, and focus on avoiding an unwanted uhd

Elementary English Course

200 Common Regular Verbs in English – Ordered by Pronunciation

Rule 1
verb ends in t = uhd

accept
admit
alienate
attempt
attract
chat
cheat
communicate
complete
correct
create
debate
distract
doubt
exist
experiment
fascinate
fit
hate
hunt
invent
invite
last
paint
point
post
print
protect
start
suggest
target
tempt
test
text
trust
visit
wait
want
waste

Rule 2.
verb ends in d = uhd

add
applaud
attend
avoid
decide
descend
end
explode
extend
fade
fold
forward
guard
include
intend
load
mend
need

recommend
record
succeed
suspend
trade

Rule 3.
verb ends in a vowel sound = d

admire
agree
allow
annoy
appear
bother
care
consider
continue
deliver
employ
empty
enjoy
enter
fry
glue
ignore
lie
matter
occupy
offer
order
owe
play
prefer
reply
share
spare
survey
tire
tour
try
weigh
worry

Rule 4.
verb ends in a voiced consonant = d

n
clean
complain
contain
determine
earn
explain
happen
imagine
join
learn
listen
loan
open

own
phone
rain
return
stain
train

z
advise
apologise
close
erase
exercise
finalise
praise
realise
socialise
suppose
surprise
use

m
charm
climb
dream
form
perform
seem
transform
zoom

v
achieve
arrive
behave
deceive
halve
improve
live
love
move
preserve
receive

l
boil
call
fill
handle
pull
travel

j
arrange
challenge
change
manage

th
bathe

g
beg

ng
belong

b
rob

Rule 5.
verb ends in an unvoiced consonant = t

k
bake
book
brake
check
kick
knock
like
lock
look
pick
talk
thank
walk
work

s
announce
fax
fix
guess
kiss
miss
notice
pass
place
promise
pronounce
replace

ch
match
reach
switch
touch
watch

sh
finish
push
rush
wash

p
help
hope
jump
stop

f
laugh

Unit 3.6 This, That, These, and Those

3.6.1 **This**, **that**, **these**, and **those** are members of a small class of words called **demonstratives**. They are function words, rather than content words, with a grammatical function. We use them to indicate the distance – in space or time – between the speaker/writer and the noun. For example:

This is my pen. *this one here*

That is her pen. *that one over there*

3.6.2 **This** and **that** are used with singular and uncountable nouns, while **these** and **those** are used with plural nouns.

	singular (1)	plural (1+)
near in space or time here / now	this	these
not near in space or time there / then	that	those

The word 'that' can be used in a contraction, e.g. **that is = that's** while the other three words cannot be contracted: this's / these're / those're are all too difficult to pronounce.

3.6.3 This and these indicate that the noun is near in space or time, while that and those indicate that the noun is not near in space or time. For example:

This is my pen and that is her pen.
my pen is nearer to me than her pen

These are my books and those are her books.
my books are nearer to me than her books.

This and these indicate **possession** – that you have something – while that and those indicate that you do not have something, for example:

'Can I borrow **those** marker pens, please?' 'Yes, when I've finished using them.'

That's my balloon flying in the sky! *you don't have it – it's gone*

We say 'not near' rather than 'far' (as the opposite of near) because the 'that/those' noun doesn't have to be *far*. It just has to be farther than the 'this/these' noun.

3.6.4 If the time is past or future – i.e. not now – we tend to use that and those:

That was a great holiday. *the holiday is finished*
That will be a great holiday. *the holiday is in the future, not now*

If we say: 'This was a great holiday', when referring to the past, it is incorrect, because the holiday is not present. Similarly, if we say 'This will be a great holiday' it is incorrect, for the same reason.

3.6.5   This, that, these, and those can be **determiners** or **pronouns**:

demonstrative determiners:	demonstrative pronouns:
before a noun, e.g.	not before a noun, e.g.
This bag is heavy.	This is a heavy bag.

We use a determiner before a noun and it gives some information about that noun. **Articles** – the, a, and an – are also determiners (see Unit 3.1). We know that 'the' indicates a specific noun, but 'this' (or the others) indicate a **more specific** noun. If somebody asked, 'Which book do you want?' we could answer 'The book on the table', but saying 'This book' – and pointing – would be much clearer. Also we don't need to add extra information about the place – 'on the table' as we would if we used only 'the'.

3.6.6   We know whether a demonstrative is a determiner or pronoun by its position in the sentence. If it is before a noun or noun phrase (e.g. this book, or this wonderful book), it is a determiner. If it is not before a noun – let's say it is before a verb (e.g. this is a wonderful book) – then it is a pronoun.

Pronoun means 'instead of a noun'. In Latin the prefix 'pro' means 'in place of' or 'in exchange for'. A pronoun replaces an unnecessary noun and makes the sentence tidier:

Not: '**This bag** is a heavy bag.'   ...but: '**This** is a heavy bag.'

3.6.7   We can add 'one' (for singular nouns) or 'ones' (for plural nouns) to the demonstrative pronoun if, for example, you are choosing something. It makes the sentence more emphatic and your choice more specific:

"I want this."
"Which one?"
"*This* one!"

"Do you like these trousers?"
"Which ones?"
"*These* ones!"

However, 'these ones' and 'those ones' are not commonly used in standard English. We prefer to say: 'these' or 'those'.

3.6.8   Although this, that, these, and those are **function words**, they are often pronounced with stress in spoken English. This is because of their function – to <u>emphasise</u> which one – and their position in a clause, which is often at the end for demonstrative pronouns. If a function word comes at the end of a clause, it is usually stressed.

Yes, I agree with that!   'that' is pronounced That (strong form)

In fact, 'these' and 'those' do not even have weak forms. They are pronounced Theez and Theuz in every context. Demonstrative determiners 'this' and 'that' can be unstressed:

That was a nice meal.   th_ w s Nai Smiyl.

Each has a weak form with a shwa sound:

	weak form (not stressed):	strong form (stressed):	notes:
this	ths	this	with a schwa sound
that	tht	that	with a schwa sound
these	-	theez	no weak form
those	-	theuz	no weak form

Students may make two common errors when pronouncing demonstratives :

- this and these both pronounced the same: theez
- failure to learn to pronounce the voiced th sound, meaning the pronunciation is more like: Dis, Dat, Deez, Deuz, or Zis, Zat, Zeez, Zeuz, rather than: This, That, Theez, Theuz

3.6.9   Common functions of this, that, these, and those:

- to specify a noun: I want this one.
- to compare two things: I like this chair, but not that one.
- to introduce somebody: This is my brother, Jack.
- to introduce yourself on the phone: Hi, this is Jane.
- to refer back to something: 'I'm going to be on time.' 'That's good.'
- before time words and phrases   This morning, this month, this evening, etc.

This week / month / year, etc. (unfinished time) contrasts with **last** week / month / year, etc. (finished time) and **next** week / month / year, etc. (future).

3.6.10   Demonstratives connect with other **pronouns** in the following way:

If singular (thing):   this / that   use: it / its / itself

If plural (thing/people):   these / those   use: they / them / their / theirs / themselves

For example:

- **This** book is great, isn't **it**.
- **That** cat is washing **itself**
- **These** books are interesting, aren't **they**?
- **Those** boys are eating **their** lunch.   etc.

Note: if the subject is singular and male or female, we use he / she etc. See Unit 4.3 for more about pronouns.

3.6.11   Remember, 'that' as a demonstrative determiner or pronoun is different to 'that' as a relative pronoun in relative clauses, e.g. 'I enjoyed the book **that** you gave me.' It looks and sounds the same, but has a different use.

Idioms corner:

this and that is an **idiom** that means: 'a few different things'. For example:

'What did you buy at the shop?' 'This and that.'
'What are you doing later?' 'This and that.'

We can use it when we don't want to be too specific.

Ex. 3.6.1   **Writing** Some of the sentences are incorrect. Write them correctly:

1. This book is good. _____
2. Those flowers were beautiful. _____
3. This books is good. _____
4. These reports is interesting. _____
5. This books are good. _____
6. Those flower was beautiful. _____
7. These reports are interesting. _____
8. That meal were lovely. _____
9. This book are good. _____
10. These report are interesting. _____
11. That meals was lovely. _____
12. These report is interesting. _____
13. That meal was lovely. _____
14. Those flower were beautiful. _____
15. That meals were lovely. _____
16. Those flowers was beautiful. _____

Ex. 3.6.2   **Writing** Write 4 sentences with this, that, these, those as a determiner:

1. _____
2. _____
3. _____
4. _____

Ex. 3.6.3   **Writing** Write 4 sentences with this, that, these, those as a pronoun:

1. _____
2. _____
3. _____
4. _____

Ex. 3.6.4   **Writing** Write 4 sentences using this, that, these, those to compare two things:

Ex. This is my pencil and that is her pencil.

1. _____
2. _____
3. _____
4. _____

Ex. 3.6.5   **Writing** Correct each sentence using a demonstrative pronoun:

1. This book is a good book. _____
2. Those seats are empty seats. _____
3. That film was an enjoyable film. _____
4. These cars are fast cars. _____
5. That game was an amazing game. _____
6. This meal is a delicous meal. _____

Ex. 3.6.6 **Reading** a) Complete each sentence with **this**, **that**, **these**, or **those**. b) Write **D** for **determiner** and **P** for **pronoun**. c) Discuss with a partner: which words in each sentence helped you to find the answer?

1. Look at _____ beautiful mountains.
2. I'm getting off because _____ is my stop.
3. I'll use _____ laptop and you use _____ one over there.
4. Who was _____ on the phone? My cousin Alan.
5. _____ meeting last night was a waste of time.
6. I need to borrow _____ book, but _____ librarian said I couldn't.
7. _____ are my favourite plants. Yes, they are lovely. I don't like _____ over there by the gate.
8. Hi Paul, _____ is Brian. Is _____ a good time to talk?
9. Who are you meeting _____ morning?
10. 'Please take another cake.' 'Is _____ the last one?' 'Yes, but you can have it.'
11. Mmm, _____ cakes look delicous. I can't wait to try one!
12. Do you remember the 1980s? Yes, _____ were the days!
13. _____ is going to be the best party ever!
14. Mmm, _____ cakes are delicious. Please have another one!
15. _____ is Joe who works in the accounts department.
16. I prefer _____ trousers to _____ in the other shop.
17. What have you been doing _____ week?
18. OK, stop. _____'s enough petrol! It's full.
19. I think I'll go to bed early tonight. Yes, _____'s a good idea.
20. 'I really hate Clive.' '_____ was a nasty thing to say, Jo.'

Ex. 3.6.7 **Reading** a) Complete each sentence with **this**, **that**, **these**, or **those**. b) Write **D** for **determiner** and **P** for **pronoun**. c) Discuss with a partner: which words in each sentence helped you to find the answer?

1. _____ classes began two months ago.
2. 'Look! _____'s my favourite actor!' 'Where?' 'Over there.'
3. _____ is a good concert, isn't it?
4. Did you go to Sally's flat yesterday? No, but I'm going _____ morning.
5. 'My grandma gave me _____ earrings.' 'They're beautiful. They really suit you.'
6. Look at _____ coin I found.
7. '_____ is a picture of my classmates.' 'They look nice.'
8. _____ kids are playing too close to the road. Go and tell them.
9. Did you watch _____ tv programme I told you about?
10. They had to sell their car. Yes, _____ was a shame.
11. I wish _____ bus would start moving. I'm going to be late.
12. _____'s my house on TV!
13. Look at _____ scar on my hand.
14. _____ class was so boring.
15. _____ guinea pigs are so cute. They're happy for me to stroke them.
16. Hi Mike. How are you? _____ are my friends Millie and Liam.
17. _____ are my horses in the video.
18. Look at _____ man over there.
19. '_____ are the last two pancakes.' 'Thanks, dad.'
20. _____ classes begin next week.

Ex. 3.6.8   **Reading** a) Complete each sentence with **this**, **that**, **these**, or **those**. b) Write **D** for **determiner** and **P** for **pronoun**. c) Discuss with a partner: which words in each sentence helped you to find the answer?

1. Were you alright during _____ storm last night?
2. _____ jacuzzi is so relaxing!
3. What are _____ kids doing over by _____ old oak tree?
4. I don't like _____ very hot weather we are having at the moment.
5. 'Who's _____?' '_____ is my cousin John.'
6. _____ jacuzzi was so relaxing.
7. _____ new trams are so cool. I can't feel _____ one moving.
8. Shall we park in _____ space or the one over there?
9. 'Have you finished exercise five?' 'No, I didn't have time for _____ one.'
10. 'Take _____ bags upstairs please.' 'Which ones.' 'The ones over there.'
11. 'Our date went really well, mum.' '_____'s nice dear.'
12. _____ is what I've written so far.
13. _____'s a nice guitar you are holding.
14. _____ bag is too heavy. I'm going to put it down.
15. 'Are you using _____ spoon over there?' 'No, I've got _____ one.'
16. Here you are – put _____ bags in the boot, please.
17. _____ shoes are so uncomfortable. I can't wait to take them off.
18. _____ who dislike classical music will not enjoy the concert.
19. _____ are my shoes on top of the cupboard.
20. _____ pullovers belong to Jenny and the other ones are mine.

Ex. 3.6.9   **Reading** a) Complete each sentence with **this**, **that**, **these**, or **those**. b) Write **D** for **determiner** and **P** for **pronoun**. c) Discuss with a partner: which words in each sentence helped you to find the answer?

1. _____ is a wonderful meal! I hope it never ends!
2. _____ gardens were so beautiful. I'm so glad I went on _____ day trip.
3. '_____ is a rare stamp.' 'What about _____ one over there?' 'Yes, _____ one is rare too.'
4. 'Look – it says _____ bridge is closed.' 'How can you read it from here?'
5. _____ pages contain gap-fill exercises, while the next page is a writing activity.
6. '_____ is my dad.' 'It's nice to meet you, Carla.'
7. 'Can I borrow _____ marker pens, please?' 'Yes, when I've finished using them.'
8. 'Let's meet at 9.30am tomorrow.' 'OK, _____'ll be great.'
9. _____ was a wonderful meal! I was hoping it would never end!
10. 'Which milk do you want in your coffee.' '_____ one. Here you are.'
11. _____ bridge was closed, so we had to turn round.
12. _____ stones have been here for thousands of years. Please don't touch them!
13. _____'s my balloon flying in the sky!
14. I'm going to see my solicitor _____ afternoon.
15. 'I forgot to set my alarm and now I'm late.' '_____ was careless, wasn't it?'
16. Hey! Who is responsible for _____ mess? _____ kids, or _____ outside?
17. Look! _____ students have got blue hair! Don't laugh – they might come over!
18. _____ suitcase was too heavy.
19. _____ trams were so uncomfortable. I won't use them again.
20. _____ gardens are so beautiful. I'm so glad I came on _____ day trip.

Ex. 3.6.10 **Writing** Write 20 sentences for your teacher to mark. In each sentence you should use a demonstrative *incorrectly*. Write WHY it is incorrect and the correction, for example:

Ex. That schools is closed. *'That' + 'schools' do not match, because 'that' is used with singular nouns and 'schools' is plural. Correction:* That school is closed.

1. _____
2. _____
3. _____
4. _____
5. _____
6. _____
7. _____
8. _____
9. _____
10. _____
11. _____
12. _____
13. _____
14. _____
15. _____
16. _____
17. _____
18. _____
19. _____
20. _____

Unit 3.7 Daily Routines

3.7.1 It is important to be able to talk about the everyday things that we do – in past, present, and future tenses. These are actions that happen regularly, so we will often need to talk or write about them.

3.7.2 In this unit we will revise and practise some of the material from three previous units, so you might want to refer back to them as you study this unit. These units are:

- Unit 2.2   5 Tenses and 5 Forms of the Verb
- Unit 2.7   Telling the Time
- Unit 3.5   Common Regular and Irregular Verbs

3.7.3 We use **present simple** (with **infinitive** and **s-form**, for he/she/it) to talk about regular actions, so we often use it to talk about our daily routine:

    I drive to work at 8am.

We can add an **adverb of frequency** like 'usually' before the verb (or after if the verb is 'be'):

    I **usually** drive to work at 8am. | I am **usually** late every Monday!

...or we could use a time phrase at the end of the sentence, for example:

    I drive to work at 8am **every day**.

3.7.4 Remember that we use **present continuous** (with **ing form**) to talk about actions that are happening now or in the future at an arranged time:

    I'm driving to work at the moment.
    I'm driving to work tomorrow.

We use **past simple** (with **past tense** form) to talk about actions in finished time:

    I drove to work yesterday.

...and **present perfect** (with **past participle** form) to talk about actions in unfinished time:

    I have (just) driven to work.

We use **future simple** (with **infinitive** form) to talk about actions in the future:

    I will drive to work tomorrow.

3.7.5 Here are some of the actions that we do every day. In the table below you will find a list of common verbs in different forms, along with examples of words and phrases that collocate (go well with) those verbs, on the right. Note how many of the verbs that we use to describe regular actions are irregular (in red). These are all phrases that you could use to talk about your daily routine. Of course, we do different things on different days. We may have one routine for weekdays (Mondays to Fridays), another for weekends (Saturdays and Sundays), another for holidays, and yet another for special occasions (e.g. your birthday / graduation, etc.).

Elementary English Course

Let's look at a typical weekday, starting from early morning and finishing at night:

irregular verbs

Morning:

infinitive	s form	past tense	past participle	ing form	example collocation
wake up	wakes up	woke up	woken up	waking up	at 7am / early
switch off	switches off	switched off	switched off	switching off	the alarm
snooze	snoozes	snoozed	snoozed	snoozing	for 10 minutes
get up	gets up	got up	got up	getting up	at 7.10am / early
take	takes	took	taken	taking	a shower / a bath
have	has	had	had	having	a wash
dry	dries	dried	dried	drying	my hair
put on	puts on	put on	put on	putting on	my clothes / make-up
get dressed	gets dressed	got dressed	got dressed	getting dressed	quickly
switch on	switches on	switched on	switched on	switching on	the radio
check	checks	checked	checked	checking	my phone / email
get ready	gets ready	got ready	got ready	getting ready	for school / work
eat	eats	ate	eaten	eating	breakfast
brush	brushes	brushed	brushed	brushing	my teeth
leave	leaves	left	left	leaving	my house / flat
travel	travels	travelled	travelled	travelling	to work / school
get	gets	got	got	getting	the bus / train
get to	gets to	got to	got to	getting to	school / work
start	starts	started	started	starting	work
work	works	worked	worked	working	hard
do	does	did	done	doing	some work
go to	goes to	went to	been to / gone to	going to	classes
have	has	had	had	having	lessons
send	sends	sent	sent	sending	an email
attend	attends	attended	attended	attending	a meeting
talk to	talks to	talked to	talked to	talking to	colleagues / friends

Afternoon:

infinitive	s form	past tense	past participle	ing form	example collocation
have	has	had	had	having	lunch
work	works	worked	worked	working	hard
have	has	had	had	having	a break
finish	finishes	finished	finished	finishing	work
leave	leaves	left	left	leaving	work
go	goes	went	been / gone	going	home
buy	buys	bought	bought	buying	a sandwich / magazine

Evening:

infinitive	s form	past tense	past participle	ing form	example collocation
get	gets	got	got	getting	home
make	makes	made	made	making	dinner
eat	eats	ate	eaten	eating	dinner
do	does	did	done	doing	the washing up
tidy up	tidies up	tidied up	tidied up	tidying up	my home
clean	cleans	cleaned	cleaned	cleaning	the kitchen
relax	relaxes	relaxed	relaxed	relaxing	at home / all weekend
enjoy	enjoys	enjoyed	enjoyed	enjoying	some free time
do	does	did	done	doing	something
do	does	did	done	doing	my homework
go out	goes out	went out	been / gone out	going out	for a drink / with friends
go	goes	went	been / gone	going	to the pub / cinema
watch	watches	watched	watched	watching	TV
read	reads	read	read	reading	a book / newspaper

surf	surfs	surfed	surfed	surfing	*the internet*
play	plays	played	played	playing	*a game*
phone	phones	phoned	phoned	phoning	*a friend / mum / brother*
get	gets	got	got	getting	*ready for bed*
get	gets	got	got	getting	*undressed*
take off	takes off	took off	taken off	taking off	*my clothes / make-up*
put on	puts on	put on	put on	putting on	*my pjs / nightdress*
brush	brushes	brushed	brushed	brushing	*my teeth*
go	goes	went	been / gone	going	*to bed*
go	goes	went	been / gone	going	*to sleep*
sleep	sleeps	slept	slept	sleeping	*all night / for 8 hours*

3.7.6   Look at the table above again and note the very common verbs that repeat a few times:

do   eat   get   go   have   put   work

It is so important that you know each form of common verbs like these. Note that they are all irregular verbs, apart from 'work':

infinitive	*s form*	*past tense*	*past participle*	*ing form*
do	does	did	done	doing
eat	eats	ate	eaten	eating
get	gets	got	got	getting
go	goes	went	been / gone	going
have	has	had	had	having
put	puts	put	put	putting
work	works	worked	worked	working

The verb 'get', in particular, is one of the most common and flexible verbs in English. It has many different meanings (see p.86), including the following in brackets:

get angry   (become)   get an email   (receive)
get the bus   (catch)   get the phone   (answer)
get a cup of tea   (make)   get there   (arrive)
get a job   (find)   get better   (recover)

3.7.7   At weekends we might do other things, for example:

<u>Weekends:</u>

infinitive	*s form*	*past tense*	*past participle*	*ing form*	*example collocation*
have	has	had	had	having	*a lie in*
go	goes	went	been / gone	going	*shopping*
do	does	did	done	doing	*some gardening*
meet	meets	met	met	meeting	*friends*
do	does	did	done	doing	*the washing / ironing*
practise	practises	practised	practised	practising	*a musical instrument*
write	writes	wrote	written	writing	*a story*
work on	works on	worked on	worked on	working on	*a project*
do	does	did	done	doing	*some DIY*
play	plays	played	played	playing	*football / golf*
have	has	had	had	having	*a party*
go	goes	went	been / gone	going	*swimming*
ride	rides	rode	ridden	riding	*my bike*
bake	bakes	baked	baked	baking	*a cake*

3.7.8   When we are on holiday we have a break from our normal routine. We may do a number of different actions, depending on where we go and what kind of holiday we have. Look at the lists of **common regular and irregular verbs** in Unit 3.5 for ideas of verbs you can use. Similarly, on **special days**, such as birthdays, festivals, and milestones (e.g. your graduation), or **unusual days** when something extraordinary happens, you will need to use a range of different verbs.

Exercises

Ex. 3.7.1   **Writing** Write 10 different times and infinitive verbs on the timelines to show what you usually do each day **from Monday to Friday**:

night / morning:

12am

12pm

afternoon / evening / night:

12pm

12am

Write 10 sentences in present simple tense, for example: I usually eat breakfast at 8am every day.

1. _____
2. _____
3. _____
4. _____
5. _____
6. _____
7. _____
8. _____
9. _____
10. _____

Ex. 3.7.2   **Writing** Write 10 sentences in present simple tense to show what you usually do **at the weekend**. For example: I usually play football at the weekend.

1. _____
2. _____
3. _____
4. _____
5. _____
6. _____
7. _____
8. _____
9. _____
10. _____

Ex. 3.7.3 **Speaking & Listening** Discuss your activities with your partner. Find out what they usually do during the week and at the weekend. Ask and answer questions in different tenses, e.g. 'What do you usually do on Sundays?' / 'What did you do last Sunday?' Then tell the whole class about your partner's activities.

Ex. 3.7.4 **Writing** Convert the 10 sentences from Ex. 3.7.1 into present continuous. Add a time phrase to make each sentence an arrangement:

Example: I'm eating breakfast at 8am tomorrow morning.

1. _____
2. _____
3. _____
4. _____
5. _____
6. _____
7. _____
8. _____
9. _____
10. _____

Ex. 3.7.5 **Writing** Write 10 sentences with past simple to show what you did yesterday:

Example: I played football in the park yesterday.

1. _____
2. _____
3. _____
4. _____
5. _____
6. _____
7. _____
8. _____
9. _____
10. _____

Ex. 3.7.6 **Writing** Convert these 10 sentences into present perfect, as if you have done them today:

Example: I have played football in the park today.

1. _____
2. _____
3. _____
4. _____
5. _____
6. _____
7. _____
8. _____
9. _____
10. _____

Ex. 3.7.7   **Writing** Write 10 sentences with future simple to show what you will do tomorrow:

Example: I will do my homework tomorrow.

1. _____
2. _____
3. _____
4. _____
5. _____
6. _____
7. _____
8. _____
9. _____
10. _____

Ex. 3.7.8   **Reading** a) Complete the sentences below using **present simple** verbs:

I _____ the newspaper at 8.00am.
I _____ a coffee break at 10.30am.
I _____ a shower at 7.30am.
I _____ a bus to work at 8.30am.
I _____ up at 7.15am.
I _____ work at 9.00am.
I _____ lunch at 1.00pm.
I _____ to my friend on the phone at 2.30pm.
I _____ an email at 2.40pm.
I _____ up at 7.05am.
I _____ breakfast at 7.45am.
I _____ home at 5.00pm.
I _____ my guitar at 9.00pm.
I _____ dinner at 6.00pm.
I _____ to bed at 11.10pm.
I _____ football at 7.00pm.
I _____ a book at 10.00pm.
I _____ to the radio at 10.40pm.
I _____ TV at 8.30pm.
I _____ the dishes at 6.30pm.
I _____ to sleep at about 11.20pm.

b) Write the sentences in the order that they happen.

Ex. 3.7.0   **Reading** a) Complete the sentences below with a different **past tense** verb form:

1. Billy _____ a book with his sister on Sunday before tea.
2. Billy _____ a dictionary in class on Tuesday at about 10am.
3. Billy _____ an argument with his sister on Sunday after breakfast.
4. Billy _____ breakfast on Monday at 7.20am.
5. Billy _____ his friend about his new dog on Friday at lunchtime.
6. Billy _____ late for school on Tuesday.
7. Billy _____ a gold bracelet in the park on Wednesday at 4.35pm.
8. Billy _____ his sister with her homework on Thursday night.
9. Billy _____ to the cinema on Wednesday evening.
10. Billy _____ around the park ten times on Saturday morning.
11. Billy _____ rugby for an hour on Monday after school.
12. Billy _____ a new bike on Thursday afternoon.
13. Billy _____ ill on Tuesday before breakfast.
14. Billy _____ his teacher a gift on Thursday at 8.15am.

15. Billy _____ a model of the Leaning Tower of Pisa on Friday afternoon.
16. Billy _____ his friend borrow his pencil on Thursday at 9.45am.
17. Billy _____ some news about his grandma on Friday at 11.25am.
18. Billy _____ his younger sister to a concert on Saturday at 3.10pm.
19. Billy _____ his house early on Wednesday morning.
20. Billy _____ a few emails on Monday after tea.

b) Put the sentences into time order, from Monday morning to Sunday evening.
c) Write a quiz based on this information, e.g. 'When did Billy...?' or 'Did Billy...?'

Ex. 3.7.10   **Reading**   a) This week Billy's mum has been on a business trip to Stockholm, Sweden. Complete the sentences below with a different **past participle** verb form:

1. She has _____ her tablet by dropping it on the ground.
2. She has _____ hard with her international team.
3. She's _____ the hotel manager for more pillows.
4. She's _____ forgetting to ask for things in Swedish.
5. She has _____ to enjoy travelling without her family.
6. She has _____ sushi for the first time.
7. She has _____ two important contracts with local builders.
8. She's _____ an open air performance of Aida.
9. She has _____ four seminars for local business leaders.
10. She has _____ on her hotel balcony and admired the lovely view.
11. She has _____ the tickets to an exciting event.
12. She has _____ the president of a local cheese manufacturer.
13. She's _____ too many cups of expensive coffee.
14. She's _____ for a celebratory meal with all her colleagues.
15. She has _____ to her husband a few times.
16. She's _____ on a terrace beside a beautiful fountain.
17. She has _____ $100 by coming third in a karaoke competition.
18. She's _____ some interesting and useful work.
19. She has _____ the city's famous art gallery.
20. She has _____ a lot to tell her family!

b) Write a quiz based on this information, e.g. 'What has...?' or 'Has Billy's mum...?'

Ex. 3.7.11   **Speaking & Listening**   Work with a partner. Using **present perfect**, tell them five things that you have done this week that are **true** and five things that are **false**. Mix up the order and ask them to guess which five things you have really done! Then swap roles.

Ex. 3.7.12   **Speaking & Listening**   a) Talk to your partner about how your routine changes when it is not a normal weekday or weekend, but rather a **holiday**, **special day** (e.g. a birthday), or an **unusual day** (e.g. you do something that you don't normally do).

b) Use your imagination and describe the daily routine of a famous person or fictional character. What do they do each day – and when?   c) Use *would* + *infinitive* to talk about your **ideal day** – what would you do if you could do anything in the world? For example: I would go shopping in Paris; then I would fly to Barcelona... and so on.

Ex. 3.7.13 **Writing** Write up your ideas from Ex. 3.7.12 as an essay, short story, poem, or dialogue:

Name: _____ Date: _____

Elementary English Course

100 Collocations and 30 Different Meanings of Get

get...

On this page there are 30 different meanings of the verb **get** (in red), not including phrasal verbs and idioms. That's why there are so many possible collocations. The most common meanings of **get** are: *achieve, acquire, arrive, become, bring, catch, receive,* and *understand*.

Literal Phrases:

- angry about sth (become)
- back (return)
- the bus (take, catch)
- Channel 5 (receive a TV or radio broadcast)
- a cold (catch)
- a criminal (catch, hold, apprehend)
- a cup of tea (bring)
- dinner (make, cook, prepare)
- divorced (become)
- sby to do sth (ask, persuade)
- a doctor (call, request)
- the door (answer)
- dressed (become)
- drunk (become)
- excited (become)
- a grade (achieve, earn, receive)
- help (call for, ask)
- home (arrive)
- an idea (receive)
- ill (become)
- in (enter, e.g. a car)
- some information (find out, discover, receive)
- a job (find)
- a letter (receive)
- lost (become)
- married (become)
- some money (receive, earn)
- a nappy (fetch, procure)
- a new book (buy, borrow)
- off (disembark, e.g. bus, train, plane, etc.)
- on (alight, e.g. bus, train, plane, etc.)
- out (leave)
- permission (ask, request, acquire)
- the phone (answer)
- pregnant (become)
- a program (download, install)
- punished (be)
- ready (become)
- a reward (receive)
- rich (become)
- a shower (have)
- started (start, begin)
- there (arrive)
- through (contact, e.g. on the phone)
- to sby (reach sby)
- together (meet)
- up (stand up, rise)
- upset about sth (become)
- used to sth (become)
- wet (become)

Idioms:

- about (travel frequently)
- across (communicate)
- your act together (improve your behaviour)
- ahead (do better in life than other people)
- at (suggest)
- at sby (annoy sby, criticise)
- away! (I don't believe you!)
- away from (avoid)
- away from it all (go on holiday)
- sth back (have sth returned)
- back to normal (return to a normal state)
- sby's back up (annoy sby)
- behind (support)
- better (recover)
- busy (become)
- by (manage, esp. with little money)
- cold feet (become unsure about doing sth)
- down (become depressed)
- down (dance)
- down to sth (begin)
- far (achieve a lot)
- the hang of sth (learn how to do sth)
- a head start (start sth before other people)
- into sth (begin liking sth)
- it (understand sth)
- it in the neck (be told off)
- a kick out of sth (enjoy, esp. sth negative)
- a life (improve your life)
- a load of sth (look at sth very interesting)
- lost! (rude way to tell sby to leave)
- the message (understand)
- your money's worth (get a fair amount of sth)
- a move on (hurry up)
- moving (start)
- nowhere (make no progress)
- off on the wrong foot (start sth in a negative way)
- on sby's nerves (annoy sby)
- on with sby (have a good relationship)
- out of sth (avoid doing sth unappealing)
- sth out of sth (gain sth useful from a situation)
- over sth (accept a negative situation, recover)
- over yourself! (don't be so self-important)
- people going (make people excited, tease)
- rid of sth (dispose of)
- the sack (lose your job)
- somewhere (make progress)
- through (survive, e.g. a difficult situation)
- to (arrive, reach)
- to sby (irritate sby)
- told off (receive a verbal warning)

Elementary English Course

Unit 3.0 Learning English:

Ex. 3.0.1   Answers will vary.

Ex. 3.0.2   Answers will vary.

Ex. 3.0.3   Answers will vary.

Ex. 3.0.4   Answers will vary.

Ex. 3.0.5   Answers will vary. Suggested answer:

not serious:	serious:	life-threatening:
cut stomach ache headache rash toothache sunburn cold	infection broken bone fever allergy migraine diabetes flu asthma	cancer HIV / AIDS heart attack Parkinson's disease leukemia

Ex. 3.0.6   See diagram on p.6.

Ex. 3.0.7   Answers will vary.

Ex. 3.0.8   Answers will vary.

Ex. 3.0.9   1. ear. 2. neck. 3. nose. 4. eye. 5. throat. 6. leg. 7. ankle. 8. foot. 9. finger. 10. arm. 11. head. 12. stomach. 13. shoulder. 14. hand. 15. chest. 16. elbow. 17. toe. 18. back. 19. mouth. 20. knee.

Ex. 3.0.10   1. spine. 2. cheek. 3. trachea. 4. forehead. 5. wrist. 6. thumb. 7. tooth / teeth. 8. brain. 9. kidney. 10. hair. 11. muscle. 12. eyebrow. 13. thigh. 14. larynx. 15. vein. 16. toenail. 17. nostril. 18. intestines. 19. bowel. 20. liver.

Ex. 3.0.11   Answers will vary.

Ex. 3.0.12   Answers will vary.

Unit 3.1 Articles:

Ex. 3.1.1   1. a. 2. a. 3. a. 4. an. 5. an. 6. an. 7. an. 8. a. 9. a. 10. a. 11. an. 12. an. 13. a. 14. a. 15. a. 16. an. 17. an. 18. a. 19. an. 20. a. 21. a. 22. a. 23. an. 24. an. 25. an. 26. a. 27. a. 28. an. 29. a. 30. a.

Ex. 3.1.2   1. a) no article. b) The. c) a. d) an. 2. a) a. b) The. c) an. d) no article. 3. a) no article. b) a. c) The. d) an. 4. a) no article. b) the. c) a. d) an. 5. a) the. b) A. c) no article. d) An. 6. a) no article. b) an. c) a. d) the. 7. a) no article. b) the. c) an. d) a. 8. a) the. b) a. c) an. d) no article. 9. a) an. b) the. c) no article. d) a. 10. a) the. b) a. c) no article. d) an. 11. a) a. b) no article. c) an. d) the. 12. a) the. b) a. c) an. d) no article. 13. a) no article. b) a. c) an. d) the. 14. a) no article. b) the. c) an. d) a. 15. a) an. b) no article. c) the. d) a. 16. a) a. b) the. c) an. d) no article.

Ex. 3.1.3   4 singular countable nouns: book, watch, clock, umbrella. 4 plural nouns: t-shirts, buses, children, socks. 8 uncountable nouns: orange juice, information, furniture, beef, work, love, rugby, transport. 4 proper nouns: Richard, Microsoft, Monday, Europe. 16 common nouns: all the words, apart from the 4 proper nouns. 7 abstract nouns: information, work, Microsoft, Monday, love, rugby, transport.

Ex. 3.1.4   1. -. 2. -. 3. -. 4. the. 5. -. 6. the. 7. the. 8. an. 9. the. 10. a. 11. a. 12. -. 13. the. 14. -. 15. the. 16. -. 17. an. 18. the. 19. the. 20. the. 21. an. 22. -. 23. -. 24. the. 25. the. 26. -. 27. -. 28. a. 29. the. 30. the. 31. an. 32. -. 33. -. 34. the. 35. -. 36. a. 37. -. 38. the. 39. -. 40. the.

Ex. 3.1.5

	Article:	Noun:	Type of Noun:	Rule:
a)	-	music	uncountable – abstract / general	8
b)	the	employees	plural / specific	5
c)	the	time	singular countable / specific	3
d)	-	chewing gum	uncountable – concrete / general	6
e)	a	film	singular countable / general / consonant sound	1
f)	-	Paris	proper	10
g)	an	app	singular countable / general / vowel sound	2
h)	-	cakes	plural / general	4
i)	the	potato	singular countable / specific	3
j)	-	Coca-Cola	proper	10
k)	the	progress	uncountable – abstract / specific	9
l)	a	car	singular countable / general / consonant sound	1
m)	the	rice	uncountable – concrete / specific	7
n)	-	children	plural / general	4
o)	an	egg	singular countable / general / vowel sound	2
p)	the	patience	uncountable – abstract / specific	9
q)	the	socks	plural / specific	5
r)	the	money	uncountable – concrete / specific	7
s)	-	perseverance	uncountable – abstract / general	8
t)	-	hair	uncountable – concrete / general	6

Ex. 3.1.6

	Article:	Noun:	Type of Noun:	Rule:
a)	the	grass	uncountable – concrete / specific	7
b)	-	Darren	proper	10
c)	-	ice cream	uncountable – concrete / general	6
d)	the	pen	singular countable / specific	3
e)	-	work	uncountable – abstract / general	8
f)	an	orange	singular countable / general / vowel sound	2
g)	the	photo	singular countable / specific	3
h)	the	dedication	uncountable – abstract / specific	9
i)	-	students	plural / general	4
j)	-	Tuesday	proper	10
k)	-	petrol	uncountable – concrete / general	6
l)	the	courage	uncountable – abstract / specific	9
m)	-	life	uncountable – abstract / general	8
n)	a	coat	singular countable / general / consonant sound	1
o)	-	colds	plural / general	4
p)	an	idea	singular countable / general / vowel sound	2
q)	the	furniture	uncountable – concrete / specific	7
r)	the	assignments	plural / specific	5
s)	a	book	singular countable / general / consonant sound	1
t)	the	chips	plural / specific	5

Ex. 3.1.7

a) 1. - . 2. the. 3. - . 4. a. 5. The. 6. a. 7. the. 8. - . 9. a. 10. - . 11. a / her. 12. - . 13. an. 14. a. 15. - . 16. a. 17. the. 18. - . 19. - . 20. - .

b) 1. E. 2. D. 3. E. 4. A. 5. B. 6. A. 7. D. 8. F. 9. A. 10. F. 11. A / G. 12. E. 13. A. 14. G. 15. E. 16. A. 17. C. 18. E. 19. E. 20. F.

Unit 3.2 SVOPT Word Order

Ex. 3.2.1   Answers will vary.

Ex. 3.2.2   Note for these pages: you could cut up the cards in any of these activities and mix them up for students to put back into order.

1. Answers will vary. Sample answers: 1. Lou. 2. his stall. 3. book. 4. to Greece. 5. her husband. 6. today. 7. Simone. 8. her daughter. 9. baked. 10. in the kitchen. 11. pictures. 12. every day. 13. Sue. 14. to Oliver. 15. charge. 16. in the office. 17. seeds. 18. yesterday. 19. The students. 20. the mess.

2. Answers will vary. Sample answers: 1. Mum. 2. the curtains. 3. damaged. 4. on the street. 5. clothes.

6. once a week. 7. Polly. 8. her suitcase. 9. met. 10. in the boardroom. 11.squirrels. 12. every day. 13. My brother. 14. me. 15. will take. 16. to work. 17. the oven. 18. later. 19. I. 20. work.

3. 1. Lenny raised his hand in class on Monday. 2. I read my book in the living room every day. 3. I'm watching a good film on my computer now. 4. Katy buys some grapes at the greengrocer's every week.
5. He's presented his paper at the university today. 6. She is wearing her watch on her right arm at the moment. 7. We have painted all the walls in our bedroom this week. 8. Penny eats her breakfast in front of the telly every morning. 9. We will meet you outside the fish and chip shop later. 10. The boys sang some lovely carols at the school concert yesterday.

4. 1. We have booked our flights to Florida this morning. 2. He has two coffees at his desk every day at 8.30am. 3. We took a taxi to the station on Saturday evening. 4. I sell charity cards in the shopping centre once a year. 5. Joe will cut my hair in the salon in a minute. 6. Stephanie asks a lot of questions in class every day. 7. A thief has stolen a handbag from my mother's car. 8. My friends carried their bags up the stairs a few minutes ago. 9. The girls wash their hair in the sink twice a week. 10. We're going to play hockey on the playing field at 2pm.

Ex. 3.2.3

1. Answers will vary. Sample answers:

	Subject:	Verb:	Object:	Place:	Time:
1.	The postman	ate	an apple	in the park	last Wednesday.
2.	Carla	has had	a massage	at the spa	today.
3.	The flatmates	are going to buy	a new fridge	for their house	tomorrow.
4.	Des	was writing down	the answers	in the exam hall	yesterday.
5.	Our cat	ripped up	a £50 cardigan	in the kitchen	last week.
6.	Scientists	will have found	intelligent life	in the universe	by 2250.
7.	Lola	is admiring	a painting	in the gallery	at the moment.
8.	Ben	parked	his 4X4	at the market	on Friday lunchtime.
9.	Simon	is going to make	some ice cream	at Lily's flat	later on.
10.	The manager	will be dealing with	any issues	in her office	at quarter past four.

2. Answers will vary. Sample answers:

	Subject:	Verb:	Object:	Place:	Time:
1.	Mrs. Jenkins	received	a few phone calls	at home	this morning.
2.	The girls	have been writing	Christmas cards	in the study	all afternoon.
3.	Theo's Donuts	announced	a new kind of filling	at a press conference	last week.
4.	Jemima	rides	quad bikes	in the old quarry	every Monday evening.
5.	Their toddler	was making	funny faces	in the restaurant	the whole time.
6.	The orchestra	had taken	a break	in the refectory	before restarting.
7.	The music app	will be downloading	the whole album	to the SIM card	while you are asleep.
8.	Our parents	will've been leading	nature walks	along remote coastal paths	for four days, by the time you arrive.
9.	Old Grandpa	has produced	some wonderful cider	in his 'secret' brewery	these past few years.
10.	Wallace	is unpacking	his clothes	in his tiny tent	now.

Ex. 3.2.4   Answers will vary.

Unit 3.3 Intonation

Ex. 3.3.1   1. a) Sentence stress is the sequence of stressed and unstressed syllables in a spoken sentence.
b) Connected speech is the group of techniques we use to connect syllables in a sentence in spoken English. c) Intonation is the way we put emphasis on different parts of a sentence, using varied pitch, volume, rhythm, etc.

2.

a) I left early │ because I didn't like the film. (↗ │ ↘)

b) It was past ten o'clock, │ so we had to go. (↗ │ ↘)

c) Jim bought some cornflakes │ and a pie. (↗ │ ↘)

d) The book was good at first, │ then boring. (↗ │ ↘)

3. a) tube. b) brother. c) three biscuits. d) remote control.

4.

a) Do you like raw fish? (↗)

b) We both enjoyed the gig, didn't we? (↘)

c) This is the right bus, isn't it? (↗)

d) What's the date today? (↘)

5. a) 4. b) 3. c) 1. d) 2.

6. a) tone of voice. b) rhythm. c) extra emphasis. d) pausing for effect. e) pitch. f) speed. g) volume.

7. a) 5. b) 3. c) 1. d) 4. e) 2. f) 6.

8. Answers will vary. Sample answers:

tone of voice	pitch	extra emphasis on content words	volume	rhythm	speed	pausing (for effect)
nervous	lower	no	quieter	broken	slower	no
surprised	higher	yes	louder	broken	slower	yes
tired	lower	no	quieter	intact	slower	no
disgusted	higher	yes	louder	broken	faster	yes

9. Answers will vary.

10. i) a) 3. b) 5. c) 1. d) 4. e) 2. f) 6.

ii) Answers will vary.

11. Answers will vary.

Unit 3.4 Past Simple and Past Continuous

Ex. 3.4.1 1. went. 2. saw. 3. watched. 4. walked. 5. came. 6. enjoyed. 7. rained. 8. drank. 9. ate. 10. had.

Ex. 3.4.2 1. cooked. 2. wanted. 3. laughed. 4. made. 5. left. 6. tried. 7. thought. 8. bought. 9. finished. 10. went.

Ex. 3.4.3 See p.47.

Ex. 3.4.4 See p.48.

Ex. 3.4.5 1. Which taxi company did you recommend? 2. Did you watch that film last night? 3. When did you start learning English? 4. Did you ask about your results? 5. Why did your boss call you this morning? 6. What did Tina say to you? 7. Did your parcel arrive on time? 8. How did your exam go? 9. Who did you invite to your party? 10. Where did the rest of the cheesecake go?

Ex. 3.4.6 1. Was the train leaving just as you arrived? 2. Were you going into the kitchen when the phone rang? 3. Were you reading funny posts on Twitter most of the night? 4. Were you thinking of inviting my mother to Tim's birthday meal? 5. Was the bee buzzing around in an annoying manner yesterday? 6. Were you always making up in-jokes about Kevin? 7. Was your uncle running a bath when the earthquake began? 8. Were the children refusing to eat their salad when grandma arrived? 9. Was the meteorite heading straight for earth when it exploded? 10. Was Lena's husband going to meet his son from a former marriage?

Ex. 3.4.7 Answers will vary.

Ex. 3.4.8 Answers will vary.

Ex. 3.4.9 1. yesterday. 2. tomorrow. 3. yesterday. 4. tomorrow. 5. tomorrow. 6. tomorrow. 7. yesterday. 8. yesterday. 9. yesterday. 10. tomorrow. 11. yesterday. 12. tomorrow. 13. tomorrow. 14. yesterday. 15. yesterday. 16. yesterday. 17. tomorrow. 18. yesterday. 19. yesterday. 20. tomorrow. 21. yesterday. 22. tomorrow. 23. tomorrow. 24. tomorrow. 25. tomorrow. 26. yesterday. 27. tomorrow. 28. yesterday. 29. tomorrow. 30. yesterday.

Ex. 3.4.10 See 3.4.5.

Unit 3.5 Common Regular and Irregular Verbs

Ex. 3.5.1 See p.57.

Ex. 3.5.2 See p.58.

Ex. 3.5.3 See p.59.

Ex. 3.5.4

regular verbs:				irregular verbs:			
want	use	seem	arrive	take	go	be	know
need	try	help	ask	have	get	think	make
call	play	work	clean	say	do	run	sing

Ex. 3.5.5 1. went. 2. brought. 3. chose. 4. got. 5. drove. 6. grown. 7. put. 8. thought, knew. 9. left. 10. swum. 11. wore. 12. stank. 13. stolen. 14. took. 15. wrote.

Ex. 3.5.6 1. woke up, heard. 2. jumped, switched off, woke. 3. switched on, was. 4. used, looked. 5. went, put. 6. got, brushed. 7. had, packed. 8. boiled, made, watched. 9. opened, picked up. 10. put on, checked, hadn't. 11. left on, knew, got. 12. unlocked, opened, went. 13. locked, walked. 14. got into, turned. 15. put on, turned up. 16. looked, reversed. 17. drove, reached. 18. sat, drove. 19. changed, tapped.

20. put on, listened to. 21. played, sang along. 22. turned, parked, turned off. 23. got out, shut, locked, walked. 24. bought, headed. 25. entered, said. 26. got to, put down. 27. was.

Ex. 3.5.7   1. be. 2. read. 3. hear. 4. see. 5. buy. 6. break. 7. eat. 8. write. 9. sleep. 10. meet. 11. find. 12. bring. 13. grow. 14. think. 15. know. 16. become. 17. drive. 18. forget. 19. leave. 20. tell.

Ex. 3.5.8   1. Meik. 2. Bild. 3. Looz. 4. Yeik. 5. Dringk. 6. Let. 7. Hav. 8. Kan. 9. Doo. 10. Kach. 11. Ring. 12. Get. 13. Fiyl. 14. Geu. 15. Puut. 16. Pei. 17. Weir. 18. Send. 19. un d Stand. 20. Flai.

Ex. 3.5.9   Answers may vary. Sample answers: 1. got. 2. had. 3. made. 4. ate. 5. went. 6. heard. 7. thought. 8. came. 9. got. 10. got. 11. rang. 12. said. 13. thought. 14. heard. 15. put. 16. ran. 17. got. 18. drove. 19. told. 20. lost. 21. said. 22. wrote. 23. rang. 24. felt. 25. knew. 26. ran. 27. was. 28. went. 29. was. 30. bought. 31. read. 32. broke. 33. got. 34. put. 35. went. 36. heard. 37. held. 38. found. 39. let. 40. slept. 41. was. 42. took. 43. were. 44. gave.

Ex. 3.5.10   A few days ago Michael Morrison **heard** a really good programme about yaks on the radio. He remembered that he once **read** a very interesting book about yaks, and he decided to buy a copy and read it again. The next day he **woke up** early, **had** a shower, **got** dressed, **ran** downstairs, **had** breakfast, then phoned his friend Mandy Minton, who **was** a zoologist, but unfortunately she didn't know about the book. Michael **put on** his coat and **went** outside. He **drove** to the library and **asked** the assistant if they **had** a copy of "Yaks of the World – Illustrated Edition". The assistant **thought** for a moment and **spent** a few minutes checking the records on his computer, but nothing **came up**.

Michael **left** the library and walked into town. He stopped at the huge bookstore on Crompton Street and **went in**. He browsed the books, but could not find "Yaks of the World" anywhere – illustrated or not. A bookseller **said** that there **was** a book called "Just Yaks", but Michael did not want it. A passing vegan **told** Michael to try a specialist bookseller on Marriott Street – a place where they **sold** unusual books. Michael thanked the lady and **paid** for a copy of "Bridge Repair Weekly" magazine. At the specialist bookstore on Marriott Street Michael **felt** sure that he would find the book he wanted, but after talking with a very quiet man in a long cardigan, Michael **understood** that they didn't have any books about yaks – or indeed any other kind of long-haired animal. He exited the shop sadly and **drove** home.

He **made** a quick sandwich and watched an excellent online video about clever llamas on YouTube. Then he **had** a bright idea: "I haven't looked online for the book yet!" He **spent** the next few hours searching for the book in online bookstores, auction sites, and forums – but without any luck. There **was** no such book as: "Yaks of the World – Illustrated Edition" "Maybe I dreamed it," he sighed to himself and **went** to bed, where he **did** in fact dream about finding the book. In his dream he **saw** it at the bottom of his wardrobe, underneath a pile of socks. When he **woke up** he looked in his wardrobe, but there **weren't** any books there. Only the socks.

A fews days later, Michael **sat down** at his computer and **began** to write the first chapter of "Yaks of the World – Illustrated Edition". After fourteen years of hard work – including many trips to the zoo – it **was** finally ready to publish and it **became** a number one bestseller – among zoologists.

Unit 3.6 This, That, These, and Those

Ex. 3.6.1   Answers may vary. Sample answers: 1. Correct. 2. Correct. 3. This book is good. 4. These reports are interesting. 5. This book is good. 6. That flower was beautiful. 7. Correct. 8. That meal was lovely. 9. This book is good. 10. These reports are interesting. 11. That meal was lovely. 12. This report is interesting. 13. Correct. 14. Those flowers were beautiful. 15. Those meals were lovely. 16. Those flowers were beautiful.

Ex. 3.6.2   Answers will vary.

Ex. 3.6.3   Answers will vary.

Ex. 3.6.4   Answers will vary.

Ex. 3.6.5   1. This is a good book. 2. Those are empty seats. 3. That was an enjoyable film. 4. These are fast cars. 5. That was an amazing game. 6. This is a delicious meal.

Ex. 3.6.6   1. Look at **those** beautiful mountains. (D) Example of words that helped: 'Look' means that I'm pointing something out; 'mountains' – if you can see mountains, plural, they are not near, so we use 'those'. 2. I'm getting off because **this** (P) is my stop. 3. I'll use **this** laptop (D) and you use **that** one (P) over there. 4.

Who was **that** (P) on the phone? My cousin Alan. 5. **That** meeting (D) last night was a waste of time. 6. I need to borrow **this** book (D), but **that** librarian (D) said I couldn't. 7. **These** (P) are my favourite plants. Yes, they are lovely. I don't like **those** (P) over there by the gate. 8. Hi Paul, **this** (P) is Brian. Is **this** a good time to talk? 9. Who are you meeting **this** morning (D)? 10. 'Please take another cake.' 'Is **that** (P) the last one?' 'Yes, but you can have it.' 11. Mmm, **those** cakes (D) look delicous. I can't wait to try one! 12. Do you remember the 1980s? Yes, **those** (P) were the days! 13. **This** (P) is going to be the best party ever! 14. Mmm, **these** cakes (D) are delicious. Please have another one! 15. **This** (P) is Joe who works in the accounts department. 16. I prefer **these** trousers (D) to **those** (P) in the other shop. 17. What have you been doing **this** week (D)? 18. OK, stop. **That** (P)'s enough petrol! It's full. 19. I think I'll go to bed early tonight. Yes, **that** (P)'s a good idea. 20. 'I really hate Clive.' '**That** (P) was a nasty thing to say, Jo.'

Ex. 3.6.7   1. **Those** classes (D) began two months ago. *Example of words that helped: 'began two months ago' – the time is not near; it is finished time (past simple), and 'classes' is plural, so we use 'those'.* 2. 'Look! **That** (P)'s my favourite actor!' 'Where?' 'Over there.' 3. **This** (P) is a good concert, isn't it? 4. Did you go to Sally's flat yesterday? No, but I'm going **this** morning (D). 5. 'My grandma gave me **these** earrings (D).' 'They're beautiful. They really suit you.' 6. Look at **this** coin (D) I found. 7. '**This** (P) is a picture of my classmates.' 'They look nice.' 8. **Those** kids (D) are playing too close to the road. Go and tell them. 9. Did you watch **that** tv programme (D) I told you about? Yes, **that** (P) was a shame. 11. I wish **this** bus (D) would start moving. I'm going to be late. 12. **That** (P)'s my house on TV! 13. Look at **this** scar (D) on my hand. 14. **That** class (D) was so boring. 15. **These** guinea pigs (D) are so cute. They're happy for me to stroke them. 16. Hi Mike. How are you? **These** (P) are my friends Millie and Liam. 17. **Those** (P) are my horses in the video. 18. Look at **that** man (D) over there. 19. '**These** are the last two pancakes.' 'Thanks, dad.' 20. **These** classes (D) begin next week.

Ex. 3.6.8   1. Were you alright during **that** storm (D) last night? *Example of words that helped: 'last night' – the time is finished (past simple), so it is logical that the storm has finished too; also 'storm' is singular, so we use 'that'.* 2. **This** jacuzzi (D) is so relaxing! 3. What are **those** kids (D) doing over by **that** old oak (D) tree? 4. I don't like **this** very hot weather (D) we are having at the moment. 5. 'Who's **this** (P)?' '**This** is my cousin John.' 6. **That** jacuzzi (D) was so relaxing. 7. **These** new trams (D) are so cool. I can't feel **this** one (P) moving. 8. Shall we park in **this** space (D) or the one over there? 9. 'Have you finished exercise five?' 'No, I didn't have time for **that** one (P).' 10. 'Take **those** bags (D) upstairs please.' 'Which ones.' 'The ones over there.' 11. 'Our date went really well, mum.' '**That** (P)'s nice dear.' 12. **This** (P) is what I've written so far. 13. **That** (P)'s a nice guitar you are holding. 14. **This** bag (D) is too heavy. I'm going to put it down. 15. 'Are you using **that** spoon (D) over there?' 'No, I've got **this** one (P).' 16. Here you are – put **these** bags (D) in the boot, please. 17. **These** shoes (D) are so uncomfortable. I can't wait to take them off. 18. **Those** (P) who dislike classical music will not enjoy the concert. 19. **Those** (P) are my shoes on top of the cupboard. 20. **These** pullovers (D) belong to Jenny and the other ones are mine.

Ex. 3.6.9   1. **This** (P) is a wonderful meal! I hope it never ends! *Example of words that helped: 'is' – the time is present – near to the subject – and 'meal' is singular, so we use 'this'.* 2. **Those** gardens (D) were so beautiful. I'm so glad I went on **that** day trip (D). 3. '**This** (P) is a rare stamp.' 'What about **that** one (P) over there?' 'Yes, **that** one (P) is rare too.' 4. 'Look – it says **that** bridge (D) is closed.' 'How can you read it from here?' 5. **These** pages (D) contain gap-fill exercises, while the next page is a writing activity. 6. '**This** (P) is my dad.' 'It's nice to meet you, Carla.' 7. 'Can I borrow **those** marker pens (D), please?' 'Yes, when I've finished using them.' 8. 'Let's meet at 9.30am tomorrow.' 'OK, **that** (P)'ll be great.' 9. **That** (P) was a wonderful meal! I was hoping it would never end! 10. 'Which milk do you want in your coffee.' '**This** one (P). Here you are.' 11. **That** bridge (D) was closed, so we had to turn round. 12. **These** stones (D) have been here for thousands of years. Please don't touch them! 13. **That** (P)'s my balloon flying in the sky! 14. I'm going to see my solicitor **this** afternoon (D). 15. 'I forgot to set my alarm and now I'm late.' '**That** (P) was careless, wasn't it?' 16. Hey! Who is responsible for **this** mess (D)? **These** kids (D), or **those** (P) outside? 17. Look! **Those** students (D) have got blue hair! Don't laugh – they might come over! 18. **That** suitcase (D) was too heavy. 19. **Those** trams (D) were so uncomfortable. I won't use them again. 20. **These** gardens (D) are so beautiful. I'm so glad I came on **this** day trip (D).

Ex. 3.6.10   Answers will vary.

Unit 3.7 Daily Routines

Ex. 3.7.1   Answers will vary.

Ex. 3.7.2   Answers will vary.

Ex. 3.7.3   Answers will vary.

Ex. 3.7.4   Answers will vary.

Elementary English Course

Ex. 3.7.5   Answers will vary.

Ex. 3.7.6   Answers will vary.

Ex. 3.7.7   Answers will vary.

Ex. 3.7.8   I wake up at 7.05am. I get up at 7.15am. I have/take a shower at 7.30am. I have/eat breakfast at 7.45am. I read the newspaper at 8.00am. I catch a bus to work at 8.30am. I start/begin work at 9.00am. I have/take a coffee break at 10.30am. I have/eat lunch at 1.00pm. I talk to my friend on the phone at 2.30pm. I send/write/read an email at 2.40pm. I go home at 5.00pm. I have/eat dinner at 6.00pm. I wash the dishes at 6.30pm. I play football at 7.00pm. I watch TV at 8.30pm. I play my guitar at 9.00pm. I read a book at 10.00pm. I listen to the radio at 10.40pm. I go to bed at 11.10pm. I go to sleep at about 11.20pm.

Ex. 3.7.9   A) Answers will vary. Sample answers: 1. read. 2. used. 3. had. 4. ate. 5. told. 6. was. 7. found. 8. helped. 9. went. 10. ran. 11. played. 12. bought. 13. felt. 14. gave. 15. made. 16. let. 17. heard. 18. took. 19. left. 20. sent. B) Time order: 4, 11, 20, 13, 6, 2, 19, 7, 9, 14, 16, 12, 8, 17, 5, 15, 10, 18, 3, 1. C) Answers will vary.

Ex. 3.7.10   A) Answers will vary. Sample answers: 1. broken. 2. worked. 3. asked. 4. kept. 5. tried. 6. eaten. 7. signed. 8. watched. 9. led. 10. stood. 11. bought. 12. met. 13. drunk. 14. paid. 15. spoken. 16. danced. 17. won. 18. done. 19. visited. 20. got. B) Answers will vary.

Ex. 3.7.11   Answers will vary.

Ex. 3.7.12   Answers will vary.

Ex. 3.7.13   Answers will vary.

Ingram Content Group UK Ltd.
Milton Keynes UK
UKHW050003040723
424501UK00006B/8